DEGREES OF EQUALITY

To the Geneva Lake Branch –

Susan Levin

IN THE SERIES

Critical Perspectives on the Past

EDITED BY SUSAN PORTER BENSON,

STEPHEN BRIER, AND ROY ROSENZWEIG

Degrees of Equality

THE AMERICAN ASSOCIATION
OF UNIVERSITY WOMEN
AND THE CHALLENGE OF
TWENTIETH-CENTURY FEMINISM

Susan Levine

TEMPLE UNIVERSITY PRESS

PHILADELPHIA

Temple University Press, Philadelphia 19122
Copyright © 1995 by Temple University. All rights reserved
Published 1995
Printed in the United States of America

Library of Congress Cataloging-in-Publication Data

Levine, Susan, 1947–
    Degrees of equality : the American Association of University Women
and the challenge of twentieth-century feminism / Susan Levine.
        p.   cm.—(Critical perspectives on the past)
    Includes bibliographical references and index.
    ISBN 1–56639–326–4
        1. American Association of University Women—History.   2.
Women—
Education (Higher)—United States—History—20th century.
3. Feminism and education—United States—History—20th century.
I. Title.   II. Series.
LB1756.L4   1995
376.8′0973—dc20   94-44693

CONTENTS

ILLUSTRATIONS
(following page 116)

1. New York City Branch of AAUW presents Woman of the Year Award to Marian Anderson, 1958. (From left) Dr. Margaret M. Bryant, NYC Branch president; Marian Anderson; and Miss Malverna Hoffman.

2. Delegates to AAUW Convention, June 1959. (From left) Mrs. W. Louis Moore, delegate from San Diego; Eleanor Roosevelt; and Mrs. Ray Townsend, from Long Beach, California, vice president of the South Pacific Region.

3. Margaret Mead at AAUW Convention (nd).

4. Coretta Scott King Award, 1969. (From left) Nell Painter; Dr. Anne G. Pannell (AAUW president, 1967–1971); and Coretta Scott King.

5. Kathryn McHale (AAUW general director, 1929–1950) (nd).

6. Mary Woolley (AAUW president, 1927–1933) (nd).

7. Meta Glass (AAUW president, 1933–1937) (nd).

8. Margaret S. Morriss (AAUW president, 1937–1941) and Helen C. White (AAUW president, 1941–1947) (nd).

9. Althea K. Hottel (AAUW president, 1947–1951) and Susan B. Riley (AAUW president, 1951–1955), April 1951.

10. Helen Bragdon (AAUW general director, 1950–1959) (nd).

11. Anna L. Rose Hawkes (AAUW president, 1955–1963), 1959 AAUW Convention, Kansas City.

12. Esther Brunauer (AAUW staff associate) (nd).

13. Kathryn McHale (wearing hat in center back) with WAC.

14. Million Dollar Endowment Trust Signing, June 1953. (From

ACKNOWLEDGMENTS

When I contracted to write this history of the American Association of University Women (AAUW) and the AAUW Educational Foundation, I had only an inkling of the project ahead. A history of the AAUW's first fifty years had been written in 1929; I was being asked to write an update that would place the organization in the context of the modern movement for women's rights. The AAUW Educational Foundation assured me that I would enjoy complete editorial freedom, provided access to several past Association board members, and allowed me unlimited use of the organization's national records.

When I arrived at the AAUW library in the Washington, D.C., headquarters, I was, to say the least, awestruck by the task ahead. Each of AAUW's national committees, most of the board presidents, many of the regional board representatives, and most of the staff associates had left volumes of material behind. The organization had been involved in an incredible array of issues ranging from consumer education, nursery schools, and support for public education to hearings on public access to television in the 1950s, the poll tax, and the intercontinental ballistic missile, not to mention the full range of women's issues, including standards for women's educational degrees and establishing fellowships for female scholars, jury service, the draft for women, affirmative action, equal pay for teachers, and the Equal Rights Amendment (ERA). The Association's archives contained enough material for several books and dissertations.

I have, of necessity, told only part of AAUW's story. The history recounted here focuses on the organization at its national level and emphasizes only those themes that seemed to me to connect AAUW to the larger world of women's organizations and liberal reform from 1929 to 1979. The local narratives related serve to amplify those themes. Although I was unable to include in this book the histories of all the branches and many crucial individuals, my appreciation of their efforts increased with each day of research.

I would like to thank the AAUW Educational Foundation for initiating this project and providing an AAUW History Fellowship to support the work. In addition, I would like to thank the AAUW Educational Foundation board members and staff who assisted me. I am especially grateful to the AAUW archivist, Dorothy Sponder, and her successor, Judy Knudsen; both were extremely helpful in sorting through vast quantities of material. In addition, Sheila Buckmaster who patiently saw the project through to publication deserves a special thanks.

A number of colleagues and friends made it possible for me to complete work on the book. A Faculty Summer Stipend from East Carolina University supported my research, and my colleagues in the History Department there lent friendship and support. Two graduate students, Kathryn Nasstrom from the University of North Carolina–Chapel Hill and Christina Greene from Duke University, generously shared their work and enthusiasm with me; I look forward to future exchanges with them. Anne Firor Scott and Susan Porter Benson each read an early draft of the manuscript and offered helpful critiques as well as invaluable support. Leon Fink read more than one draft and offered his usual wit and insight to the project. Although I willingly take responsibility for the information and arguments presented here, this book owes its existence to these colleagues.

No one writes in a vacuum and I am particularly fortunate in having a circle of friends who make my historical work a pleasure and who constantly remind me that the relationship between history and politics need not be abstract. Mike and Melva Okun have been true friends. Their wise advice saved this project at a crucial moment. Jacquelyn Hall has been a steady support for many years, as have Mary Frederickson, Judith Bennett, and Cynthia Herrup. Susan Porter Benson has been both a colleague and a friend. Our shared interests have spanned consumerism, the women's movement, and our children's adolescence. I look forward to our continued conversations.

In the end, it is my family, immediate and extended, to whom I owe the most. Family members have consistently encouraged my work and have given me the love that makes it all worthwhile. The Pawleys' Group lived closely with this project for two summers and never let me lose confidence. Anna and Simon made sure that I kept my sense of perspective. Leon, in addition to being an intellectual partner, can still make me laugh. It is to him that I dedicate this book.

Susan Levine

INTRODUCTION

Looking back in 1931 on a half-century of work, two founders of the American Association of University Women (AAUW) observed, "The Association's pride is that it has been a part, through fifty years, of a great movement for human civilization especially as it relates to women."[1] Their sentiments reflected the pride and accomplishments of a generation of pioneers. AAUW represented the nation's first women with higher education degrees, the first women to become college administrators, deans, and professors, and the first women to venture into professional careers. It was the first organization to monitor conditions for women in American colleges and universities and to promote legislation designed to further women's educational opportunities. Finally, AAUW was the only organization that offered young women concrete financial assistance for their education through its long-established fellowship program. AAUW members believed that women could, if artificial barriers to equality and opportunity were removed, ensure the nation an expert, rational, and democratic leadership.

The Association's second half century, 1929–1979, witnessed major transformations in AAUW membership, in its structure, and in its relationship to the American women's rights movement. AAUW and the AAUW Educational Foundation secured a prominent place among national women's organizations with their unique emphasis on equity in education, equal opportunities in professional careers and public service, and equal rights in law and politics. Believing that education provided the key to equality in a democratic society, AAUW members sought ways to enable women to reach their individual potential, become leaders in their communities, and participate in the nation's collective, political life. Through their fellowships, AAUW and the Educational Foundation had a national impact on women's scholarship and promoted their belief in the infinite capacity of the female mind. Through its myriad committees and programs, AAUW also sought to shape public policy. Representing the ever-expanding group of women who received college degrees and sought equality in employment and political life, AAUW laid clear claim to the ideological mainstream within the American women's rights movement.

The history of AAUW and the AAUW Educational Foundation since 1929 provides a window on the development of the women's rights movement in the United States and the transformations in American feminism. Conventional wisdom in American women's history assumes that the women's movement declined during the 1920s as the "new woman" followed her individualistic pursuits, that it revived slightly during the Great Depression with a renewed appreciation for women's social work, and that it all but disappeared during the 1950s with the intense postwar search for domestic security only to be "reborn" with the modern feminist movement of the 1960s. Because AAUW and other major national women's organizations, rejected the label of feminist and long opposed the Equal Rights Amendment (ERA), historians, and contemporary feminist activists have regarded these organizations as largely irrelevant to the story of women's rights.

AAUW's history suggests the need for a reexamination of both the feminist label and the fate of the women's movement. If, as historian Nancy Cott has suggested, feminism contains three "core components"—an opposition to hierarchies based on sex, a belief that gender is socially constructed, and the assumption that women form a common social group—then the history of major national women's organizations provides important insight into the nature of American feminism.[2] The mainstream national women's organizations (including AAUW) did not disappear, become silent concerning gender-based discrimination, or abandon their interest in broad-based social reform after suffrage, nor did they "rediscover" feminism during the 1960s. Rather, AAUW's history suggests that women's organizations pressed for equal rights and confronted discrimination throughout the twentieth centuy, expanding their base of support and their influence in academic and legislative circles. Indeed, during the 1950s, the period during which the term *feminism* was most unpopular, AAUW's membership increased and contributions to the AAUW Educational Foundation exceeded all expectations. The spectrum of women's rights believers included not only a core of self-identified feminists but also a surprisingly large number of ordinary women. The ebb and flow of feminism might be better understood not so much as a result of changes in the objectives of women's groups but rather the result of transformations in the larger political climate in which women could pursue their goals, changing organizational and political strategies, and shifts in the language used to describe women's aims.

If the goals of women's organizations remained remarkably consistent, the context in which they could be pursued changed dramatically. American feminists and the major national women's groups that eschewed the term tied their fates to larger social reform movements, the expansion of education, and the extension of democratic rights. During the Progressive Era, women's groups shared with liberal reformers the assumption that women could bring a particularly civilizing or domesticating influence to public life. They also shared the belief that public policy was best developed by those with expertise and advanced education. By the 1930s, women's organizations and liberal reform movements generally looked to positive government actions to ensure the common welfare and safeguard individual rights. Women also assumed they would be recognized for their contributions to social reform and rewarded for their intellectual and professional achievements. Through the years of depression, war, and economic boom, women optimistically hailed public support of the expanding educational system and sought to eliminate barriers to advanced degrees. Yet, even as women articulated general principles of opportunity and equality, liberal America only reluctantly opened its doors to even its most ardent champions. Finding themselves continually barred from the institutions they most valued, women's groups such as AAUW turned in the 1960s and 1970s to new strategies and a more visible, aggressive agenda.

This volume thus assumes a double purpose. First, it tells the story of a remarkable organization that was established to encourage women to pursue higher education, pressure institutions to make women's degrees equal those of men, and ensure a broader degree of equality for women in American society. In tracking one organization's history, however, this book necessarily explores the history of the larger American women's movement as it developed in mid-twentieth-century American society. It examines the problems that bound women together, the culture they built within their organizations, and the political strategies they developed to pursue equal rights.

The narrative divides the history of AAUW, and of the larger women's movement into three periods. Between 1929 and 1945 AAUW consolidated its national headquarters in Washington, D.C., and became an important resource center for educational policy and women's concerns. The culture that had characterized women's organizations during the early years of the century endured into the World War II years as women both sought out female-centered voluntary associations and continued to be barred from male-dominated social and political institutions. During the Depression and the war years, many women were convinced that their contributions would be rewarded with recognition in the public sector. During this period, women also exerted an important influence in the international arena. Although AAUW allied with the majority of other women's groups that opposed an ERA and shied away from using the term *feminist,* the organization was convinced that women could serve their country equally with men and even advocated a military draft for women during World War II.

During the postwar period, 1945 to 1960, AAUW and the women's movement in general faced serious challenges to the presence of women in public service and the professions and to the very culture of the women's movement. A cold war climate of suspicion and fear shaped political discourse and particularly questioned women's organizations in its attack upon dissent. Women's groups, like liberal reform groups generally, retreated into a politics that avoided conflict. This cold war caution was accompanied by a popular antifeminism and a real crisis in women's education. AAUW and other women's groups found themselves questioning women's status during a period in which such questioning appeared not only unpatriotic, but, according to expert opinion, could be psychologically damaging as well. Despite this popular antifeminism, however, AAUW continued to build its fellowship funds, founded the AAUW Educational Foundation, and amassed unprecedented private support for women seeking degrees in higher education. Many women shunned the label feminist, but they continued to advocate for opportunities in education, the professions, and public life. Finally, after World War II, demands for racial integration challenged women's organizations to examine the degree to which they practiced equality within their own ranks. Although they historically articulated a universalistic language of equal rights and opportunities, women's groups traditionally represented a rather narrow, elite constituency. The movement for racial equality forced AAUW and other groups to bring their social practice into line with their political principles.

Finally, between 1960 and 1979, American feminism was not so much reborn as it was reinvigorated with increasing numbers of women gaining access to higher education, professional careers, and opportunities for public service. Challenged to maintain their historical constituency—women who might now pursue personal ambition or public service through mainstream institutions—traditional women's organizations such as AAUW began to embrace new strategies of legislative action and grassroots political organizing. During these years AAUW became a major player on the national feminist scene, adopting an activist legislative agenda and a program of grassroots mobilization and leadership training. AAUW's goals of gender equity both within and beyond educational institutions fit well with the era's search for equality. The Association's history as a voice of moderation attracted mainstream women who believed that American democratic institutions could—and would—extend equality to all. By the 1970s those women proudly adopted the term *feminist* to describe their goals.

A COMMUNITY OF EDUCATED WOMEN: 1881–1929

In November 1881, seventeen women gathered at the Massachusetts Institute of Technology (MIT) to jointly consider their future prospects and form a national organization of female college graduates.[3] Called together by Marion Talbot, a recent Boston College graduate, and her mother, Emily, also an educated woman, the group represented a unique gathering of American women. They were young, most having been out of college for fewer than five years, and all had stepped out of the social norm. Few women in the late-nineteenth-century United States went to college and even fewer pursued advanced degrees.[4] M. Carey Thomas, who later became president of Bryn Mawr College, remembered, "Before I myself went to college I had never seen but one college woman." Upon hearing that "such a woman" was visiting a neighbor, Thomas went to see her, fully expecting to see "hoofs and horns." "It was a great relief," she wrote, "to find this Vassar graduate tall and handsome and dressed like other women." When Thomas later left home to study in Leipzig her mother told her "my name was never mentioned to her by the women of her acquaintance. I was thought by them to be as much of a disgrace to my family as if I had eloped with the coachman."[5]

Each of the women, like M. Carey Thomas, had pursued an education despite warnings that it would make them ill suited for a proper female life. Contemporary theories of female education, promoted most notably by Harvard physician Edward Clark, held that intellectual activity, particularly the pursuit of higher education, would have a detrimental effect on women's health and well-being.[6] Marion Talbot recalled "the opinion prevalent, well-nigh universally, that young women could not, except at a price physically not worth while, undergo the intellectual strain which their brothers seemed to find no strain at all."[7]

The women who met in Boston had found, to the contrary, intellectual challenge and stimulation in the life of the mind. Convinced that "physiology could be transcended," they founded the Association of Collegiate Alumnae (ACA).[8] Its ambitious mission was to ensure the value of their degrees, help extend the privilege of higher education to other women, and help educated women fit into a community that would come to recognize their talents and potential.

ACA founders were confident that their new organization would attract others like themselves. Indeed, two months after the organization was founded, in January, 1882, sixty-five women answered their call. With their purpose to "unite alumnae of different institutions for practical educational work," the women embarked on a program that would alter the status and the world of female college graduates. One of the Association's first projects was a study designed by Marion Talbot to prove explicitly that college women were no less healthy than other American women.[9] The study found that college women did, indeed, suffer from "constitutional weakness" and emotional strain, but the researchers attributed the conditions to cultural expectations rather than biological limitations.[10]

Around ACA's intellectual activities, the women spun a web of formal as well as informal relationships. A constitution and bylaws governed the organization's membership and dues policies, the selection of officers, and the relationship between branches and a national board of directors. Within ten years, the Association merged with its sister organization, the Western Association of College Alumnae, and devised an elaborate network of branch, regional, and state divisions. In 1897 the Association hired its first salaried secretary-treasurer and began regular publication of a journal.[11] The following year, the Association was incorporated under Massachusetts state law.

As the Association's formal structure grew and centralized,

its membership base expanded. By 1899 almost three thousand women belonged to branches throughout the country. The earliest branches emerged in cities and regions with large concentrations of women college graduates. Washington, D.C., New York City, San Francisco, and Philadelphia branches constituted the initial core of Association membership. In 1903 southern women established a separate but parallel Southern Association of College Women.[12] By 1907 women had organized thirty-five branches throughout the East, Midwest, and West. In 1900, for example, the Minneapolis branch boasted 100 members devoted to "practical educational work" and cooperating "with the national organization in every possible way."[13] According to one account, by the turn of the century, the ACA had become "a major support for the new academic women."[14]

ACA provided concrete support for women's education by establishing scholarships to enable young women to attend college. In 1888 the Western Association's first fellowship enabled Ida M. Street to attend graduate school. Within two years the ACA's newly established Committee on Fellowships began to raise funds for permanent programs for domestic and European study. ACA branches also awarded their own fellowships, establishing endowments to support local applicants.[15] Association fellowships addressed the needs of female students that educational institutions virtually ignored. In 1884, for example, Cornell University made only one fellowship open to women, and Columbia explicitly excluded women from applying for the best fellowships.[16] ACA awards supported Yale University's first female Ph.D. and the first woman admitted to the laboratory of the United States Fish Commission. Helen Thompson, whose psychological theories would later refute prevalent notions about women's intellectual capacities, received an ACA fellowship to pursue her studies in Europe.[17]

ACA funds were also committed to generally improving the facilities and climate for women's education and, in particular, to ensuring high standards in women's education. The Association's policy of limiting membership to graduates of schools approved by its board stemmed from the conviction that the prestige that came from meeting ACA membership standards would pressure colleges and universities to raise their standards for female students. After receiving "numerous requests from institutions to join our group," one early board member commented, "It was decided that a membership policy, based on demonstrated institutional qualifications, would serve as a more effective lever to raise the standards of higher education for women."[18] This decision put the Association board in the position of evaluating and approving (or rejecting) some of the nation's most prestigious colleges and universities. As some women's colleges were rejected for being no different from finishing schools or even high schools, the ACA expected that pressure from irate graduates would force the schools to develop more rigorous programs.[19]

Although the board initially approved some institutions on purely social grounds or to strengthen local branches, setting approval standards soon became a major project. No longer would pressure from individuals wanting to bring their friends into the organization or from branches (such as the Chicago branch urging approval of Northwestern University) outweigh other considerations. The requirements for admission quickly tightened, moreover, and the Association leadership soon strongly opposed an open membership, fearing that such a policy would dilute their ability to influence the quality of women's education. In 1889 the board charged a newly appointed special Committee on Admission of Colleges with implementing new admissions requirements for institutions; colleges would be admitted only if the faculty were "not called upon to give preparatory instruction," admission requirements matched those of colleges already on the list, and they each year awarded at least twenty-five degrees to women in the arts, philosophy, science, or literature.[20] The designation of these traditional academic fields reflected the Association's initial distrust of vocational degrees and even of the professional training women received in law and medicine.[21] Rather, they sought for women a traditional liberal arts education.

The question of institutional recognition went to the heart of the Association's identity and purpose. In 1891 the ACA secretary said,

"The time has come when we must choose between working for the individual good of as large a number within the Association as possible and holding the standard of collegiate education for women so high that the influence of the Association may be felt not only by all college women, whether within the Association or not, but by all collegiate interests in the country."[22] The Association's first standing committee on corporate membership, chaired by the University of Chicago's first dean of women, Alice Freeman Palmer, outlined the rationale for strict admission standards. First, institutions were invited to join "for the educational strength" they could bring. Admitting weak institutions would condone and perpetuate the deficiencies in women's education. Second, institutions were invited to join "for the benefit of educational standards *in the whole country and not for local influence.*" That is, the Association intended to establish itself as the national guardian of standards for women's higher education.[23]

The academic standards for women in college generally were lower than those for men. After late-nineteenth-century experiments with coeducation gave way to fears that the presence of women might make programs seem less rigorous to prospective male students, public and private institutions reverted to sex-segregated programs.[24] Separate facilities and instruction also meant different course offerings and graduation requirements. Most programs for women, for example, required domestic studies in addition to the regular academic training, which at many schools was less rigorous for women. The ACA's hesitation regarding the "value" of women's degrees was well founded.[25]

The ACA's Committee on Corporate Membership revealed the Association's definition of what constituted an education appropriate to women's intellectual capabilities. Entrance and graduation requirements had to be the same for women as for men. An institution had to demonstrate a commitment to treat its women faculty and staff equally with its male employees, not only by paying women and men equally if their training was similar, but also by employing women "in proportion to the number of students." Finally, the institution had to have a solid financial base so that, for example, the dean of women would not need to raise funds to support her students.[26] The Association's interest clearly focused on the quality of the educational climate for women students, faculty, administrators, and members of boards of trustees. As Marion Talbot put it, "If women were not to be fed at a second table, so to speak, a body of women of standing and achievement organized together must stand back of the pioneers who were still working for the greatest possible intellectual achievement for women."[27]

Women college graduates constituted a powerful force in the nation's public life during the early years of the twentieth century.[28] Through their branch projects, study groups, and research, ACA women established a framework for public-policy problem solving that would characterize the Association throughout the twentieth century. Like most Progressive Era reformers, ACA women believed that social problems were rooted in environmental causes and that informed public opinion combined with expert leadership could produce rational solutions. Furthermore, they believed that educated women had a special responsibility to focus their talents on problems of social welfare, equity, and justice. Attracting considerable public attention, the ACA sponsored studies addressing standards for women's education and employment, the role of government in sponsoring vocational and public schools, and the status of women in college and university administrations. The Washington, D.C., branch's study of the status of women in the Civil Service, for example, uncovered a wealth of data demonstrating discrimination against women in government employment.[29] Branches pressured their Congressional representatives to establish pensions for teachers and to support public schooling. Chicago branch members Susan Kingsbury, Sophonisba Breckinridge, Edith Abbott, and Ellen Richards all participated in a study on "The Living Wage for College Women," which became the basis of a campaign to improve employment standards for women on the nation's college campuses.[30]

ACA branches engaged in "practical education" as well as research. The Washington, D.C., branch, for example, undertook a "sanitary inspection of the public schools"; the New York City branch monitored the state legislature's actions affecting public schools and contributed materials to start the College Settlement's library. The San Francisco branch established and supervised the city's first playground and assisted in a survey of housing conditions. The Durham, North Carolina, branch, working closely with the Young Women's Christian Association (YWCA), undertook a study of local "social betterment" agencies. Chicago's ACA, led by Marion Talbot, who had become Dean of Women at the University of Chicago, regularly funded a resident at Jane Addams' Hull House settlement house and worked with labor reformer Florence Kelley in developing the Illinois Consumers' League. Branches also pressured local colleges and universities to appoint women to administrative positions and boards of trustees. The San Francisco branch, for example, was instrumental in creating a dean of women position at the University of California and supported the selection of Phoebe A. Hearst as the first woman on the university's board of regents.

ACA members, like many other women activists of the Progressive Era, turned their energy toward government service during World War I. Although some reformers, including Jane Addams, opposed U.S. involvement in the war, others used their experience in social reform, political activism, and organizational efficiency to become major organizers in the domestic war effort. Association members, in particular, used the war effort to demonstrate women's abilities in public service. Within days of America's entry into the war, the ACA offered all of its "forces" for the war effort. M. Carey Thomas joined Mount Holyoke president Mary Woolley and Barnard president Virginia Gildersleeve (both of whom became dedicated pacifists after the war) on the Association's War Service Committee, which undertook public education "as to the causes of the war and how the United States had come to take a part in it."[31]

Local ACA branches formed speakers' bureaus to work for the Council of Defense and organized War Savings Stamp campaigns, Food Conservation campaigns, and Liberty Loan drives in their communities. ACA members across the country organized public information drives, financed ambulance units, worked in "liberty bread shops," and maintained clubhouses for soldiers.[32] The Durham branch moved its meetings to the Red Cross headquarters and combined their regular business with "hemming slings for the soldiers."[33] The Association's activities during World War I largely shaped its direction during the interwar years. Hundreds of Association members served on local and national commissions, boards, and agencies. Members led women's councils of defense and chaired relief commissions. Their intense experiences in public service strengthened their belief that women deserved equal representation—and the vote.[34]

As a result of their wartime experiences, many national women's organizations entered a phase of consolidation. In 1921, for example, recognizing the need for a more centralized organization, the ACA invited the Southern Association of College Women to join in creating a national American Association of University Women (AAUW). According to the minutes of the Durham, North Carolina, branch secretary, the southern branches were greeted with "cordiality" and welcomed the opportunity to ally with a visible national women's organization.[35] The newly united Association voted to levy yearly dues of two dollars, earmarking twenty-five cents of the dues for fellowship funds.[36] In addition, the Association hired an educational secretary and established a Committee on Educational Policy, a Committee on Standards, and a Committee on International Relations. In 1925 AAUW began holding biannual national conventions. The conventions became a major focus of Association activity and were the members' forum for endorsing policy issues and directing the board's activities for the coming years.[37]

The purchase of a national headquarters building in 1921 symbolized the organization's consolidation, and the location of the ivy-covered clubhouse two blocks from the White House, at 1634 Eye Street, reflected AAUW's growing presence in the women's political community of Washington. Demonstrating the Association's prestige in education circles, "college presidents, deans of women, heads of special departments throughout the United States," attended the headquarter's formal opening in 1922.[38] Maintained by the Washington, D.C., branch under agreement with the Association, the headquarters became a source of pride for AAUW women throughout the country. Members visiting the nation's capital were assured a friendly reception and comfortable, inexpensive accommodations. At the cost of one and a half to three dollars per night, members could stay at the clubhouse and meet women from all over the world. In addition, members from Washington could entertain guests in the clubhouse dining room.[39] Like the all-male private clubs of the era, the headquarters provided AAUW women with social and professional contacts. Women's alumni groups supplied comfortable furnishings and books for the reading rooms. Goucher's alumni, for example, donated furnishings for a reading room while the graduates of Elmira College provided a sitting room.[40] With the clubhouse and a professional staff, the development of standing committees, and the establishment of biannual conventions, AAUW became a mature national organization devoted to equality in education, law, and political life and to providing leadership in community affairs and public policies.

THE WOMEN'S MOVEMENT AFTER THE VOTE:
PEACE, EQUALITY, AND PUBLIC WELFARE

In 1920, women constituted more than 47 percent of the nation's college students. Although this percentage declined over the next three decades, the actual number of women attending college increased steadily. Where only 3.8 percent of American women aged eighteen to twenty-one attended college in 1910, the figure was 7.6 percent in 1920 and 10.5 percent in 1930.[41] Despite their increased numbers, however, women college graduates continued to face a dichotomy between professional training and society's expectations that women would have domestically centered lives. The predominantly female voluntary organizations were the one arena in which women seemed able to combine their professional training with their sense of social responsibility. The national women's organizations, including the YWCA, the Business and Professional Women's Association (BPW), the AAUW, and League of Women Voters (LWV), had consolidated in the suffrage campaigns and aimed to provide avenues through which women could use their skills, gain recognition for their achievements, and find the support and friendship of others like themselves while working for social reform. Educated women provided the natural constituency for organizations devoted to self-improvement (including women's rights) and community service. They also provided the natural constituency for a continued interest in women's rights.

World War I and the passage of the Nineteenth Amendment in 1919 marked a turning point for the American women's movement. Some historians have argued that feminism declined during the 1920s as the intense focus on suffrage dissipated. Others point to the pervasive individualism of the twenties and argue that professional women, in particular, became less interested in social issues and more concerned with personal advancement. These characterizations, however, fail to recognize that women's organizations grew and prospered and that new women's associations were formed in this period. Convinced that the vote simply provided a "long-needed tool" with which women could continue the "mothering, as it were, of all humanity," women's organizations held tightly to the Progressive Era tradition of positive government, expert leadership, and rational discourse.[42]

Although most women's organizations agreed that women's special role as "social housekeeper" need not preclude equality in the public sphere, they were bitterly divided over how to achieve equal rights after the vote. Conflict within the women's movement during the 1920s and the following decades focused largely on the ERA, which was introduced in 1921 by Alice Paul and the National Women's Party (NWP) in an effort to ensure legal equality and provide a strategic focus for the women's movement. Most women's organizations disliked Paul and the NWP's strident rhetoric and strongly opposed the ERA, fearing that the amendment would threaten hard-won legislation protecting women in the workplace.

In 1920, veteran suffrage activists led by Carrie Chapman Catt organized the League of Women Voters specifically to counter the NWP.[43]

Reflecting the conflicts in the women's movement generally, AAUW members were divided in their opinions of the ERA. Hesitating to commit the organization to a stand, the board commissioned two well-known members, M. Carey Thomas and Mary Van Kleeck, to develop a policy statement on the issue. Thomas and Van Kleeck proposed to "offer an outline of study" and suggested that AAUW serve "as a center for the exchange of information." The organization, they felt, could best serve women's interests by stimulating "a process of study" about the amendment.[44] Many members felt that AAUW would "step out of its path" if it took a position on the ERA and feared asserting "an opinion which may alienate some of its members altogether and would certainly leave many apathetic."[45] In the AAUW Journal Thomas and Van Kleeck wrote, "As university women we are probably all agreed on certain rights that we wish to secure for ourselves and other American women . . . [but] American women are not yet agreed among themselves as to the best method of securing equal rights for women." They suggested that the Association adopt a general statement endorsing the principles of social, political, and economic equality but stopped short of endorsing the ERA.[46]

As LWV and other national groups allied against the ERA, relations among the major national women's organizations became strained, if not acrimonious. NWP members, for example, who also belonged to AAUW vowed to quit and refused to contribute to the Association's fund-raising efforts if it did not endorse the amendment.[47] Veteran women's rights workers and social reformers opposed the ERA not because they rejected the idea of equal rights but because they believed that the amendment would threaten those special protections, particularly health and safety regulations, that they had worked so hard to establish.[48]

Although many histories of feminism have focused on the debate over the ERA, neither before 1919 nor after did women's groups (other than the NWP) confine their view of feminism or of women's rights to that issue. Women's organizations continued to pursue an agenda that included women's rights, social reform, health, and welfare. In 1920 the major national women's groups of the post-suffrage era united in forming the Women's Joint Congressional Committee (WJCC) to promote women's interests in federal legislation. Governed by two principles—that strong government action informed by expert advice could mitigate social problems and that women's involvement could bring an important and unique element to public policy—the WJCC became a highly visible lobbying force in Washington politics.[49] Its agenda advocated measures such as the Sheppard-Towner Infant and Maternal Health Bill, the Cable Act (establishing women's citizenship rights in international marriages), a constitutional amendment banning child labor, and the establishment of a children's bureau and a federal department of education.[50] With a legislative agenda echoing that of the WJCC, AAUW provided research, sent speakers to congressional hearings, and opened its Washington clubhouse for meetings and conferences.[51]

During the 1920s, women's groups also cooperated in an international peace movement. In 1921 AAUW's International Relations Committee sponsored the founding of the International Federation of University Women (IFUW). That same year Jane Addams and other pacifists launched the Women's International League for Peace and Freedom (WILPF). Also during that decade, the major national women's organizations, including AAUW, the YWCA, the Women's Trade Union League (WTUL), the General Federation of Women's Clubs (GFWC), and LWV, established departments or committees focusing on international affairs. In 1924, in an effort to coordinate the efforts of the various women's groups, Mary Woolley (who later became president of the Association) and veteran suffragist activist Carrie Chapman Catt launched the National Committee on the Cause and Cure of War (NCCCW), which became a "clearinghouse for peace initiatives." Advocating alternatives "acceptable to a broad range of women," the NCCCW promoted international study, sent women observers to world danger spots, and advocated for the establishment of a world court to settle international hostilities.[52] The women's groups also pressed governments to appoint women to international boards, commissions, and conferences. AAUW, for example, pressured President Warren Harding to appoint "a well qualified woman lawyer" as adviser to the American delegation to the League of Nations Codification Conference at the Hague.[53] According to one account, women's peace groups "accepted an undergirding assumption of the liberal peace movement, that vital domestic policies—or in their version, expectations for women's advancement and security—could not be accomplished under the threat of modern, total war."[54] The women's groups assumed that just as women could bring a sense of social justice and morality to domestic policy, they could provide a civilizing force in the international arena.

Virginia Gildersleeve and Mary Woolley, AAUW's preeminent international representatives, articulated most clearly women's special role in the peace movement. Born in 1877 into a wealthy New York family, Virginia Gildersleeve belonged to a "social class that frowned on career women." Ignoring family friend Mrs. John Jacob Astor's question, "Why on earth would a girl want to go to college?" Gildersleeve earned a baccalaureate degree from Barnard and a Ph.D. from Columbia. Two years later, in 1903, she became the dean of women at Barnard, where she transformed the curriculum from that of a finishing school to a solid academic program. She also introduced a course on personal hygiene, including sex, for freshmen and did not object to women smoking. A strong promoter of women's rights, Gildersleeve turned her attention to international relations and the role of women in the peace movement during World War I.[55]

The work of Gildersleeve and her colleague Mary Woolley inspired the Association's international program focused on education, research, and the role of women in international negotiations. Along with other women's groups, AAUW worked to change the status of women in international law. Under existing international laws, a married woman automatically assumed her husband's citizenship; thus, an American woman automatically lost her citizenship if she married an alien, and any children born abroad were required to take their father's citizenship. The law also specified different naturalization requirements for men and women. In 1922 women's groups united to achieve passage of the Cable Act, which allowed American women to maintain the status of naturalized citizens when they married citizens of other countries.[56] In the international arena as well as in domestic matters AAUW supported the policy of "no distinction based on sex."[57]

As AAUW approached its fiftieth year, Marion Talbot and her colleague Lois Kimball Mathews Rosenberry chronicled the Association's development. Its history, they wrote, had been "contemporaneous with the development, not only of the higher education of women, but also of great and fundamental changes in the Nation and among nations."[58] The Association had, indeed, become a significant national organization. In 1929, its membership stood at 31,647 and spanned 475 branches.[59] Twenty-three national staff members worked in the Washington headquarters. Association property was estimated to be worth more than two hundred thousand dollars and its fellowship fund totaled nearly as much.[60] Aurelia Henry Reinhardt, formidable president of Mills College and AAUW president from 1923 until 1927, did a great deal to increase the organization's coffers. She supplemented members' dues with the proceeds from a corporate funding campaign. In 1926 she secured an annual grant of five thousand dollars for five years from the Carnegie Foundation, specifically earmarked for international relations, and four years later the funds were increased to ten thousand dollars. In 1927 she negotiated a hefty grant of twenty-seven thousand dollars from the Laura Spelman Rockefeller Memorial to fund a permanent secretary and assistant. That grant doubled two years later, and through the early 1930s AAUW continued to receive smaller annual grants from the Rockefeller Memorial. The Rockefeller funds, along with the new two-dollar membership dues, enabled the Association to support its growing staff, begin a series of publications, and expand its fellowship program.[61]

By 1929 AAUW was granting more than fourteen thousand dollars annually in fellowships to women, and branches awarded an additional twenty-five thousand dollars annually in scholarships to undergraduate women.[62] Affirming its commitment to the support of women's education, the Association's Committee on Fellowships declared "in no uncertain terms its faith in the power of women to advance knowledge."[63] One of the Association's most concrete programs, the fellowships were also among its most frustrating because the numbers of women seeking assistance far exceeded its funding abilities. In 1929, for example, the Association was able to fund only 11 of the 150 women who applied for fellowships. To address this problem, the Association's 1927 convention launched a Million Dollar Campaign to establish a national fellowship endowment. Headed by Minnesota Fellowships chair Dorothy Bridgman Atkinson (later Dorothy Atkinson Rood), the campaign consolidated fellowship efforts and generated the Association's first major national fund-raising effort. Dorothy Bridgman Atkinson, the daughter of a college president, graduated from Wellesley in 1910 and while not pursuing graduate work herself, became actively involved in encouraging and enabling young women to attend college. As a Wellesley College trustee during the 1920s, she helped establish funding programs for foreign women. Her most ambitious effort resulted in Wellesley's Mayling Soong Foundation, named in honor of the Chinese student at Wellesley who shortly after graduating became Madam Chiang Kai-shek.[64]

The Million Dollar Campaign became a central feature of the Association's fellowship program for the next two decades. Carefully crafting a campaign that would generate enthusiasm and loyalty among branch members, Atkinson divided the Association into geographical units and asked each unit to commit to raising sums as high as forty thousand dollars. Despite the Great Depression, Atkinson was confident AAUW women would contribute. Because the Association did not have the resources in its Washington headquarters to support such a campaign, Atkinson set up operation in her Minneapolis home. Her husband, a Minnesota businessman, contributed his own secretary to the effort, and, according to Rood, "a very personal feeling developed" among the committee members.

By the end of the 1920s, AAUW had clearly outgrown its structure. Calling for a headquarters director and secretary and another secretary for international relations, Mary Woolley, then president of AAUW, commented, "No president who has another full-time job, as most of us have, can possibly do for an organization like this what ought to be done."[65] Woolley also urged the board to consolidate the Association's programs and strengthen its national standing. In 1929 the board appointed Kathryn McHale as its first general director.[66] The appointment proved an extremely significant act, for McHale remained at the helm, shaping AAUW policy, for the next twenty years.

Like many AAUW women, Kathryn McHale came from a middle-class family. She was educated in Logansport, Indiana, public schools and then traveled to New York City to attend Columbia University. After briefly teaching school in Logansport, she returned to Columbia, where she received a Ph.D. in psychology in 1926. With her degree in hand, McHale took a job on the faculty of Baltimore's Goucher College.

The limits of women's advancement in academic circles convinced McHale to accept AAUW's offer of employment. Board member, Mrs. A. W. Cooper, assured her that the job would be strictly professional rather than social in nature. Suggesting the title of "Director," Cooper said there should be "no doubt that the person bearing it is the active head of the organization."[67] Board president Mary Woolley agreed. (Apparently as a result of confusion about McHale's preference for her title, the title became known as "General Director.") Woolley told McHale, "The Board was anxious to do what they could to make the position attractive to you."[68] McHale accepted the position at a salary of six thousand dollars per year.[69] Under her stewardship the organization quadrupled in membership and established both a comfortable financial base and a national reputation as a source of high-quality research and reasoned policy positions.

Working at AAUW allowed McHale to shape an influential organization of women and to pursue her own professional interests. During her tenure as General Director, she continued her academic research and writing, acted as an advisor to numerous government and private commissions, served as a member of Purdue University's Board of Trustees, and took part in various national and international conferences. She also led a group of women students on European tours each summer. Under McHale's leadership the AAUW's Washington headquarters became a focus for Association activities and a national center for women's political action.

With its commitment to equity in education, equality for women, and internationalism, AAUW became a major national women's organization during the 1920s. Set apart from other women's organizations by its central focus on education and the professional training of its members, AAUW pursued feminism in its own way. Although its members were committed to ensuring equal opportunities for women in education and public life, they continued to hold to the belief that women were different from men. They chose the company of women in their political associations and many devoted considerable amounts of time and money to women's organizations. Representing a visible force in women's education and in the professions, the Association was a key player in the postsuffrage women's political movement. In addition to helping young women gain access to education, it provided a supportive community and an organization through which women could apply their education and talents to improve the general welfare. AAUW's focus on equality of opportunity for women as civic leaders, professionals, and social reformers continued a well-established strain of American feminism.

Part I

EQUALITY WITH A

DIFFERENCE: EXPERTS

IN A LIMITED SPHERE,

1929–1945

In 1931, as AAUW celebrated its fiftieth anniversary, economist and veteran Association member Susan Kingsbury proudly declared AAUW, along with the Business and Professional Women's Association and the League of Women Voters "one of the three great associations of women in the United States."[1] Indeed, these three national women's organizations represented a large group of professional women who were increasingly wielding their influence in public circles. Articulating a confidence in informed public action and a belief in the potential of government to solve the nation's social problems, members of these organizations enthusiastically accepted the challenges of the Great Depression and the opportunities offered by the New Deal administration. AAUW women, in particular, felt uniquely positioned to combine women's special sensibilities with rational public discourse. The organization's emphasis on equity in education and its reputation for quality research and moderate leadership gave it a quiet stature in an era of social crisis.

The Association's educational mission distinguished it from other national women's organizations and made it a unique resource for policy makers and educational associations. Further, the Association afforded women college graduates a professional, organizational identity and greatly increased their professional contacts. These two factors—commitment to educational equity for women and the potential for increased professional contacts—created a powerful combination that attracted ever-increasing numbers of women to the organization. Yet the Association's dual purpose, being at once a source of personal ties and an agent of social change, also defined its deepest conflicts.

Chapter I

EDUCATION AS A

BADGE OF SERVICE

The generation of college women who came of age during the 1930s entered a public world that differed in important ways from the one met by women graduates earlier in the century. The college women of the Depression era had become less of an anomaly and during the 1920s the traditional women's professions including nursing, teaching, and social work expanded. In addition, some traditionally male professions such as medicine and law had slowly opened a few doors to women members. However, with the economic crisis of the 1930s those openings began to disappear and professional women actually lost ground. Women continued to be closed out of leadership roles in their careers or chosen disciplines. For professional women of the 1930s then, organizations such as the AAUW continued to play an important role in providing professional recognition, a vehicle through which women could contribute to community life, and an important source of personal support and friendship.

AAUW members during the 1930s constituted a relatively homogeneous, but at the same time maverick, group. They were, by and large, daughters of the middle class, often educators or other professionals. Whereas earlier college women often eschewed marriage, those who graduated during the 1930s generally did not.[1] However, marriage posed two problems for the women. First, they had to try to find a "practical value" for their education, as their postcollege lives were often defined by home and family rather than the professional or intellectual pursuits they had followed in college. Excluded from many professions and jobs, educated women often turned to voluntary associations and women's organizations, fashioning alternative career paths through these groups. Second, those educated women who chose to pursue careers faced the continuing tension between their family responsibilities and their work lives. Custom and law often explicitly excluded married women from jobs, including, in many American towns, teaching. Consequently, many professional women chose to remain unmarried, live and work in female-centered communities, and choose professional and intimate associations with other women.

The AAUW membership reflected important changes in the lives of professional women during the Depression years. Opportunities for women in many professions and in academia contracted with the economy. In 1938, AAUW published a study by Susan Kingsbury showing considerable discrimination against women, particularly those who were married, in access to professions and in salary rates. Whereas more than 14 percent of the nation's professionals were women in 1930, that figure dropped to just over 12 percent in 1940. Corporate firms did not hire women executives; medical and law schools set strict quotas on the number of women allowed into their programs and greatly limited the number of internships available to them upon graduation. In addition, the institutionalization of standards and certification in fields ranging from medicine to social work disfranchised many women already working in those areas.[3] AAUW membership profiles for the late 1930s reflected the continuing restrictions on women's employment. Most of the Association's professional members could be found in traditional female occupations; more than two-thirds were educators and most of the remainder worked as librarians, social workers, health care professionals, and home economists.[4]

Although historian Nancy Cott and others have argued that interest among professional women in feminism declined during the 1920s as opportunities slowly opened in public life, women's organizations continued to thrive.[5] They provided an important source of intellectual and professional contact as well as a vehicle through which women could influence public life. AAUW, in particular, gave educated women recognition denied them by male-dominated professional associations. Its members shaped it into an alternative professional association with both the content and the trappings of professional life. Association leaders, for example, were expected to hold advanced degrees, and, indeed, most enjoyed prestigious posts as college presidents or deans of women. During these years, board members regularly donned their academic regalia for convention processions and receptions, and the Association headquarters resembled a research institute as much as a political organization.[6] According to Mary Woolley, the Association's structure was intended to resemble that of a university. The role of general director, she said, "corresponds roughly to that of college president while the national president's duties are more like those of a chairman of a board of trustees."[7]

Kathryn McHale proved to be an energetic and visionary general director. She was instrumental in expanding the Association's national office as well as its reputation in national policy making and research. Immediately after assuming her post in 1929, McHale began to consolidate the Washington office and focus the Association's far-flung branch activity in the national headquarters. In an open letter to Association members in 1932, she urged women to recognize the value of national membership in addition to their branch allegiance, and that same year the Association moved into its larger, Eye Street headquarters.[8] With money from the newly instituted national dues, McHale began publication of the organization's major internal newsletter, *The General Director's Letter,* in July 1933. Through the newsletter and her other actions, and with the support of Association founder Marion Talbot, McHale passed along to Association members her belief that women should realize "they are members of a national organization."[9]

During the next three years McHale oversaw the development of several board committees, including the Committee on Membership and Maintaining Standards, the Social Studies Committee, and the Committee on the Economic and Legal Status of Women.

In 1937 she reorganized the Committee on Legislation, and the following year the board established the Committee on the Arts.[10] By the mid-1930s the Association had sponsored 1,723 study groups in more than 600 branches; the correspondence, remarked McHale, was "tremendous."[11]

Under McHale's leadership AAUW's national headquarters became a center for women's political action. Women's groups, educational associations, international relations committees, and scores of other groups used the facilities for meetings and social gatherings. One of McHale's main tasks was to reorganize the headquarters office staff and consolidate the Association's research and publication activities. The new headquarters staff developed resource materials, research guides, and study aids for AAUW branch use, conducted research projects, and collaborated with numerous other educational, women's, and reform organizations on research and lobbying. The Association quickly developed a reputation for producing high-quality professional materials, for which there was a growing demand. In 1933, for example, the Carnegie Foundation's Wilfred Shaw labeled the AAUW's adult education materials the "prototype" in their field, and in 1935 seven AAUW publications were listed among the year's best books in the educational community's prestigious journal *School and Society*.[12] AAUW publications found their way into government programs as well. For example, in 1935 the staff of the National Emergency Council of the National Recovery Administration ordered fifteen hundred copies of AAUW's kit on "Scientific Consumer Purchasing" to use in its programs.[13]

McHale's skills in organization building and the sense of professionalism she passed on to the Association members meshed well with the Depression era's climate of public activism. She was convinced that AAUW members, because they were educated and because they were women, had a special responsibility to guide public policy. She told Association members, "There are major problems today that only a trained group can attack; we are for this reason in the most strategic position of all 31 national women's organizations."[14] Her view was shared by Association board members. In

1933, newly elected board president Meta Glass told the members, "Because we are college and university women we can justly be expected to play a sane, intelligent, well balanced part [in] and thus to be valuable interpreters of the National activities in our own communities." As educated women, AAUW members saw themselves as uniquely able to contribute to the public debate and, as Glass put it, "uphold a standard above that for the general citizen."[15]

Meta Glass served as Association president from 1933 to 1937, portraying a combination of professionalism and reform-mindedness that was common to women educated during the Progressive era. Born in Petersburg, Virginia, to a liberal southern family, Glass graduated from Randolph-Macon, one of the South's premier women's colleges. After receiving a Ph.D. from Columbia, she served during World War I with the YWCA in France and then pursued a career as a Latin scholar. Despite her family connections, however, Glass found it difficult to advance in the academic world as a female scholar. Like many women of her generation, she turned instead to academic administration. This path proved successful, and in 1925 she became president of one of the South's other prestigious women's colleges, Sweet Briar.[16] She applauded the growth of the Association and further expanded the scope of its programs. AAUW's advocacy, she observed, represented new opportunities for educated women and challenged them to make new contributions as well. "Diversity within well-defined interests," she argued, would make the organization a dynamic force in public affairs.[17]

McHale made a point of recruiting AAUW leaders who represented high academic standards and elite schools. When historian Margaret Morriss accepted the presidency in 1937, she told McHale, "I was surprised that they wanted anyone as unimportant as I am." McHale reassured her by saying, "The Association has had its eye on you, so to speak, for some time."[18] Morriss came to AAUW through Goucher connections, as McHale had. Born in Baltimore in 1884, Morriss received her undergraduate degree from Goucher in 1904 and her Ph.D. from Bryn Mawr in 1911. After study at the London School of Economics, Morriss secured an appointment in American history at Mount Holyoke just before World War I. Like Meta Glass, Morriss supervised YWCA recreational work for nurses in France during World War I. After the War Morriss became Pembroke College's dean of women. She retained that posistion for the rest of her professional life, overseeing the college's ambitious building program and presiding over a growing student body.[19]

Morriss's concern with professional standards reflected an important element in national women's organizations during the 1930s. Most women's groups, like AAUW, believed in an elite egalitarianism that rewarded educational achievement with expanding access to professional and public life. According to Nancy Cott, the American professional "credo" that individual merit would be judged and rewarded according to objective standards played an important role in shaping women's organizations during this period.[20]

Depression era cutbacks, however, threatened women's faith in that credo. Women were often among the first to be fired despite their credentials and achievements; similarly, women's programs in the nation's colleges and universities were often early victims of economic contraction. AAUW accreditation thus became an important tool for shaping educational policy for women and ensuring the maintenance of high standards. AAUW women were convinced that only with an education equal to that of men could women prove their intellectual and professional potential. Through the Committee on Membership and Maintaining Standards, established in 1933, the Association set minimum standards of admission and graduation requirements for women's education and for the status of women in faculty and administrative positions. The Committee on Membership and Maintaining Standards monitored undergraduate degree programs, evaluated facilities for women students, and pressured colleges and universities to upgrade the status of faculty women. For many years the Committee also acted as a semi-official accrediting agency, examining institutions in detail and passing judgment on their suitability for inclusion on the AAUW list.

The Committee on Membership and Maintaining Standards articulated for the Association and the public a complex set of qualifications for women's higher education. These standards included specific course requirements and distributions; minimum standards for classroom and dormitory facilities; suitable rank, status, and salaries for women faculty; and the representation of women on boards of trustees. The monumental task of monitoring this information was assigned to one of the Association's first paid staff members, hired specifically to work with the Committee on Standards. In 1930, the Association's approved list included 194 schools in the United States and another 100 abroad.[21]

Institutional candidates for the Association's approved list ran a gauntlet of requirements. In this period, the Association's standards emphasized equal recognition for women in administration, equal access to material resources, and equality in faculty status and degree requirements. Committee members carefully examined every aspect of institutional life to evaluate the type of experience women students might expect, the value of their degrees, and the treatment of women staff members. Association women particularly worried that institutions offering degrees to women maintain the same standards as those offering degrees to men. Consequently, for an institution to be on the Association's approved list, all members of its teaching staff had to hold degrees from colleges in good standing, and "a distinctly large proportion of the full professors [had to] hold degrees based on graduate university work." Its admission requirements had to include at least four years of "serious secondary school work," and its graduation requirements had to "correspond to the amount of work ordinarily included in four years of serious college study."[22] AAUW fought against a specialized vocational curriculum, pushing instead for women to receive a liberal arts education equivalent to that being developed for men.

The Association's standards established a crucial source of professional identity for AAUW members and a kind of exclusivity in the organization. But AAUW also implemented an early form of affirmative action, as they required institutions to make special provision to ensure that qualified women would be recognized.

An equally important source of recognition for women scholars was provided by AAUW fellowships and scholarships. Few other resources existed to support young women's college education and most agencies funding graduate research concentrated on male applicants. The Guggenheim foundation, for example, one of the major national research funding agencies, gave few of its scholarships to women. During the first eleven years of its existence, this major national research funding agency gave only 11 out of 525 grants to women scholars.[23] In 1936, although women made up almost one quarter of the foundation's applicants, it bestowed only 13 percent of its awards on female scholars.

AAUW fellowships, on the other hand, specifically honored women's scholarship, and branch scholarships encouraged young women to pursue educational goals. In addition to the national fellowship campaign, state divisions and local branches raised money to fund their own fellowships. In 1933, for example, the South Atlantic Region raised thirty thousand dollars for a fund named after Elizabeth Avery Colton from North Carolina's Meredith College.[24] Recognizing the obstacles to women's advanced study, AAUW women took a personal interest in each fellow. General Director Kathryn McHale even suggested that the Association raise "scholarships for the children" to provide living expenses for mothers who chose to pursue their studies.[25] By 1930, the Association regularly awarded fourteen thousand dollars per year in graduate fellowships and more than twenty-five thousand dollars in undergraduate scholarships. According to one member, fellowships were "the material expression of our confidence in women."[26] By 1936 the Association was more than one-quarter of the way toward its million dollar fellowship goal and had awarded six fellowships from income on contributions to the fund.[27] That same year AAUW received eighty-five applications for its four domestic fellowships, prompting national fellowship endowment chair Dorothy Atkinson to say that she eagerly anticipated completion of the giant fund drive "so that we shall not have to say 'no' to so many gifted women."[28]

Throughout the 1930s many women had held conflicting professional and gender identities. AAUW women and others held great respect for the social authority of academic credentials and insisted that women's abilities be recognized equally with men's, yet they also believed women were different from men. Women, they maintained, had unique sensibilities stemming from their maternal role and their domestic experiences. These special responsibilities set women apart from men. In their estimation, however, the differences by no means implied inequality. Said one graduate of the 1930s, "Our college professors taught us to be *women* with all the social graces and these alone prepared us for leadership in our communities."[29]

During the 1930s, women's organizations combined the functions of social clubs, service organizations, and political pressure groups. Including luncheons or dinners with their business meetings and regularly sponsoring programs celebrating formal or festive occasions, these organizations provided opportunities for women to develop social ties. These connections drew the members together and at the same time, fostered a homogeneous and often elite atmosphere. In addition to objective membership standards, women's organizations also had unspoken social standards. The BPW, for example, required that new recruits be recommended by established members. Some AAUW branch membership committees often went far beyond ascertaining whether prospective members held the requisite degree. They required recommendations from other members, sometimes visited the prospective member's home, and easily excluded women they deemed unsuitable or ineligible. Other groups such as the YWCA and LWV operated under much less formal membership requirements, but these groups too limited their membership largely to middle-class white women. By interest and by social networks, the natural constituency for women's organizations remained relatively small during these years.

AAUW branches reflected the dual nature of the Association as a social club and an agent of social change. Most active branches sponsored monthly dinner or luncheon meetings that generally covered business matters and then proceeded to consider special topics, often with guest speakers. The topics typically reflected AAUW standing committees such as International Relations, Fellowships, Education, The Arts, and The Status of Women. The Durham, North Carolina branch, for example, began its 1935–1936 schedule with an October meeting in which Elizabeth Gilmore, instructor in Fine Arts at Duke University, spoke on "The Attitude of National Socialism, Fascism, and the New Deal toward Art and the Artist." In November, Robert S. Rankin, a professor of political science at Duke, spoke on "Marriage and Divorce Laws in the United States." Spring speakers included a recipient of an AAUW fellowship discussing "My Experiences While Studying in Paris on an AAUW fellowship," and a guest from Vassar speaking on her school's "unique experiment in the field of adult education." The April meeting was always reserved for a tea for Duke University senior women during which members encouraged them to continue their education and join the Association. In addition to the monthly meetings, the branch supported several study groups and sponsored community projects designed to raise funds for the Association and for fellowships and to provide community services. The Durham branches and others worked with local public libraries, city schools, and citizens advisory groups.

During the 1930s women did not shirk from public leadership. In fact, most women's organizations were spawning grounds for community activists and professional pioneers. Women were convinced that, given the opportunity, they could provide rational, responsible social leadership. AAUW women, as college graduates, felt they had a responsibility both to enable younger women to take advantage of educational opportunities and to put their education to "practical use."[30] As Mary Woolley saw it, the Association helped women promote "the practical value of research."[31]

Educational standards and policy provided a natural arena of advocacy for AAUW women. The economic crisis of the 1930s threatened not only educational standards for women, but also their access to public education and to women's employment as teachers. Throughout the country, schools cut back on staff and materials, closed buildings, and in some towns ceased operating altogether for large parts of the year. Branch members who had actively promoted public schools and lobbied extensively on the state level to expand access to education saw their efforts crumble for lack of funds. In 1934 Kathryn McHale sounded the alarm in her *General Director's Letter*, noting, "Schools, libraries, and other community service institutions have been allowed to close or suffer through the curtailment of facilities at a time when they are most needed."[32] McHale warned AAUW members to "be alert . . . to the crisis in education, know the facts about your state schools and safe-guard education by sending well-informed lobbies to your capitals." The Association's national office, she assured members, stood "ready to help any state with the facts pertaining to the conditions of the school situation."[33] North Carolina members, for example, eagerly took on the task and "carefully monitored" their state legislature's 1934 budget debates. When the legislators cut school funds from forty-two thousand to sixteen thousand dollars, the North Carolina branches elicited data from principals, teachers, and parents "to bring pressure on the next session."[34]

The Depression also threatened women's professional status as teachers and educators. Women, particularly those who were married, were often the first to fall victim to tight budgets and economic hard times. By the mid-1930s, discrimination against women in both public and private agencies reached crisis proportions. McHale commented, "Like a rising tide, the subject of discrimination against women increases relentlessly in importance."[35] A 1938 NEA survey found that in more than three quarters of the cities studied no married women could be hired as teachers, and almost half of the cities required women teachers to resign if they chose to marry.[36]

Association leaders during the early 1930s envisioned women as major players in shaping public policy, particularly in the area of education, and the New Deal expansion of government provided important opportunities for women to exert their influence. AAUW and other women formed networks in Washington to exert a quiet but distinctive influence on government policy and public opinion.[37] Their approach reflected a confidence in informed public action and a belief in the potential of government to solve the nation's social problems. Schooled in the social reform mode of the Progressive Era, AAUW members advocated government action to ensure opportunity and safeguard the general welfare. Reflecting their belief in the abilities of informed citizens to shape public policy, Meta Glass said, "No service is more vital to national life at this moment than disinterested study and activity. If AAUW promotes this attitude among intelligent women at work for the betterment of national life, it alone would be almost enough."[38]

Nourished by members' beliefs that they could affect national policy and improve the general welfare, women's organizations remained healthy during the Depression years despite setbacks in the professions. AAUW membership actually grew during the 1930s, a phenomenon that General Director Kathryn McHale attributed to the "vitality we have shown in establishing and maintaining national culture."[39] The greater role of government, she suggested, gave educated women increased public responsibilities. "The future," she said, "calls for interest on the part of better trained citizens in public affairs and in the determination of public policies." McHale, like other AAUW members, was determined that women be recognized for their role in that process.

Chapter 2

TESTING THE BOUNDARIES

OF LIBERAL FEMINISM

Women's groups eagerly took up the challenge of overseeing the nation's welfare during the Depression years, convinced that women were particularly suited to for the task and that women would receive appropriate public, academic, and professional recognition for their achievements. If women's groups focused less specifically on "women's issues" and more generally on public welfare, they none-the-less felt that as women, they brought a special perspective to public life and international politics. Still, as the economic crisis threatened women's gains in employment and public life, equity became an increasingly salient issue. If the NWP pursued equal rights in the form of the ERA, other women's groups continued to press for equity in education, employment, and public service. AAUW women, in particular, developed a liberal women's ideology during the 1930s and 1940s that emphasized achievement and equity. For AAUW, a female identity went hand in hand with a broad humanitarian vision. In her annual report to the Association board, Kathryn McHale noted, "With a greater role of government [comes] greater responsibilities for our better colleges and universities and therefore for their graduates who constitute AAUW."[1] Underlying AAUW women's liberal feminism was a self-confidence and commitment to public service that accompanied individual achievement.

Historian Susan Ware argued that three aspects of the New Deal helped expand opportunities for women in public life. The crisis atmosphere allowed for experimentation and encouraged women as well as men to take an active role in solving public problems. In addition, the Roosevelt administration felt it beneficial to draw on the expertise of women in social welfare and other professions when developing the new bureaucracies. Finally, Eleanor Roosevelt provided a powerful personal example, and Franklin Delano Roosevelt displayed an unprecedented openness to women's participation.[2] Women's long experience in voluntary associations, particularly those concerned with education, children, and public welfare, made them well suited to advise the new administration. In turn, their work in public service influenced the shape of their organizations. Groups such as AAUW increasingly professionalized and expanded their national offices and lobbying efforts.[3]

Responding to the atmosphere in the Capitol, McHale nurtured the Association's legislative program and urged AAUW women to play a more visible role in "practical research." "College women have been trained to understand the significance of national and international events," she said, "but it is one thing to watch their development passively and quite another to share in them completely."[4] McHale, her growing staff, and a few other prominent AAUW members became familiar faces in legislative hearings and congressional offices, where they lobbied for the familiar women's agenda including health, welfare, and consumer affairs. In 1934 the AAUW was among a dozen organizations on the Consumer's Council pushing for consumer education, surveying the quality of milk and other products, and pressing for purity in food processing. In addition, AAUW pushed to expand and enhance public education at all levels. Joining the NEA and other educational organizations, the AAUW opposed pay cuts for teachers, promoted vocational education programs, and lobbied for a federal office of education.[5] "Personally," McHale confided to board member Georgette Waters, "I believe that legislation for the first time in our history has become important. We find that we can get so far with our study work and that is of no consequence unless there is some overt action in guaranteeing the standards desired."[6]

In most communities and on Capitol Hill, women's groups acted in concert on a number of issues. Through the wjcc and local coalitions, women formed an important lobbying force for social welfare, education, and international peace issues. Women in AAUW branches cooperated with various groups on local projects, some related to the role of women in the community and others more general in nature. The Durham, North Carolina branch, for example, worked with the YWCA and the LWV. The Durham branch's most elaborate ongoing project, begun during the mid 1930s, was a community nursery school. Spearheaded by dynamic branch member Mrs. F.A.G. Cowper, AAUW supported the nursery school until well into the 1950s.[7]

During the 1930s AAUW continued to represent a moderate feminism, particularly with regard to the ERA. The Association officially sponsored speakers both for and against the amendment, but the members of the organization remained sharply divided on this issue. The NWP's reputation in Washington made it difficult for other women's organizations to seriously consider supporting the amendment. Shortly after Kathryn McHale became AAUW's general director, the National Women's Party invited her to speak about the Association's educational program. The Washington AAUW branch was, at the time, embroiled in the controversy between the National Women's Party and the League of Women Voters, which vigorously opposed the ERA. The Washington AAUW branch told McHale that "under no circumstances" could she accept an invitation from the National Women's Party. The "rather bad situation" was politely resolved, McHale remembered, when Association president Mary Woolley "requested my presence elsewhere on the day when the Woman's Party program was scheduled."[8]

AAUW's opposition to the ERA in no way signaled a retreat from feminism. Setting themselves apart from the NWP's brand of feminism, the members of a 1934 AAUW panel advocated "a new feminism that draws the egalitarian ideal into a larger synthesis of political economy and so roots it deeper."[9] AAUW strove to develop a mainstream feminism that combined equal rights with intellectual achievement and public service. In her column in the *General Director's Letter* entitled "Some Feminist Notes," McHale opposed the NWP's claim to the term *feminism*.[10] To enhance AAUW's credibility in defining a moderate feminist politics, she convinced the board to reactivate the Committee on the Economic and Legal Status of Women (CELSW). She anticipated that the committee would provide the Association board with the "expert advice" it needed to actively oppose the ERA and would enhance AAUW's influence in the community of national women's organizations and the larger sphere of public policy. AAUW, McHale argued, was "not interested in equality on any stagnant scale" but rather was interested in building "a future status for women that grows out of doing a worthwhile job which must command respect and status."[11] In McHale's view, women's equality would be meaningful only if it was based on earned achievement; equality based on legal decree was not enough.[12]

McHale realized that the battles over women's rights were increasingly being played out in terms of the ERA and urged the Association board to develop alternative strategies. She worked quietly to ensure that the newly reconstituted CELSW would share her definition of feminism. To that end, she selected AAUW board member Susan Kingsbury, whom she felt would be open to influence from the anti-ERA women, to chair the committee.

Her choice was wise, for Kingsbury became an influential speaker for AAUW's mainstream feminism. The daughter of a woman dean, Susan Kingsbury was raised on a college campus. In 1890 she received her A.B. from the University of the Pacific, where her mother worked and began her career as a teacher. In 1905 she completed her doctorate at Columbia and went on to earn two LL.D. degrees. She joined AAUW shortly after graduating from college and within a few years became a national leader. As an AAUW board member, Kingsbury was an outspoken advocate of women's rights.[13] Although she was not unalterably opposed to the ERA when she became chair of the CELSW, she became a vocal opponent of the amendment within a few months of working with McHale. In 1937 she led the committee to recommend that AAUW officially oppose the ERA "as a means of securing equality for women in this country."[14]

By staking out a position in clear opposition to the ERA, the AAUW, in effect, declared open conflict with the National Women's Party. The NWP quickly mobilized its forces, putting pressure on women who held membership in both organizations to influence AAUW to change its position. The National Women's Party went so far as to send a representative, Helena Hill Weed, to AAUW headquarters to examine old minutes, hoping that she would find something to establish the unconstitutionality of the board's action. NWP members threatened to disrupt the AAUW convention, discredit its leadership, and provoke unflattering headlines in the press.[15] McHale maintained that the majority of AAUW members opposed the ERA and counseled the CELSW to ignore the NWP's tactics.

AAUW, under McHale's leadership, remained staunchly opposed to the ERA, even as other women's groups began to soften their stands. Some groups held that the New Deal labor legislation would provide women with sufficient safeguards for industrial protection, and by the end of the 1930s a number of women's groups, including such professional groups as the BPW, the American Medical Women's Association, and the National Association of Women Lawyers, reversed their stand on the ERA. Other professional and labor groups, however, including AAUW, the LWV, and the WTUL, continued to oppose the amendment.[16]

Regardless of their position on the ERA, women's groups during the 1930s agreed on the need for equity for women in the public sphere. They also shared the belief that equal rights for women could be attained through hard work, study, and service. For these women, important differences in sensibilities, culture, and social roles divided the women's sphere from the male world. Difference, they insisted, however, did not imply inequality. By availing themselves of educational opportunities and proving themselves capable in professional capacities, women could achieve equality and could demonstrate their capacities for social leadership. Thus, opportunity and merit were the key elements in their vision of progress and equity.[17] AAUW's McHale observed, "Women in their special concern for human relationships and human welfare have a special contribution to make. But how can that contribution be fully expressed in our national life if women are denied positions of leadership?"[18]

Women were not unaware of the subtle barriers to their participation in public and professional life. As women who had pursued the nontraditional path of higher education, AAUW members, in particular, were painfully aware of the barriers, small and large, preventing women from realizing their full potential. CELSW chair Susan Kingsbury stressed to Association members that discrimination could take subtle as well as obvious forms. She cautioned them to "watch for use of the generic term 'he' " and urged them to lodge "an appropriate protest" when it was used. Language was particularly important to women in education, Kingsbury argued, because fellowship announcements used the generic "he" even though they were open to both men and women. "As a result," she feared, "women sometimes fail[ed] to apply, thinking themselves ineligible."[19] Extending this concern, the AAUW member in charge of public relations for the Durham, North Carolina, branch reported that her greatest problem was getting others to consider AAUW members "as persons instead of women." What women want, she said, "is equal space with other civic and educational organizations. Instead we have been relegated to the Department of Tapers and Imported Lace Curtains."[20]

A key element in the strategy of most women's groups during the 1930s included advocacy for women's representation in the public sphere. In particular, the network of women activists surrounding Roosevelt's New Deal administration actively promoted women's participation in policy discussion and on public boards and commissions. Women's groups urged Roosevelt to appoint women to advisory posts and public offices. A coalition of women's organizations, for example, supported FDR's appointment of Frances Perkins as the first female cabinet member. They also joined forces to lobby for the appointment of Florence Allen, a U.S. Court of Appeals judge, to the Supreme Court. Although unsuccessful in this effort, women did make notable gains in public and appointive office during the 1930s.[21]

Like members of other women's groups, AAUW women believed that the barriers to women's achievements could—and would—be removed as women increasingly proved their worth in the public arena and pointed out the inequities that existed. Consequently, the Association promoted the appointment of women whenever they were qualified and monitored the public arena to ensure their recognition. Stressing the importance of advocating for women at every opportunity, Kingsbury advised AAUW women to be vigilant in seeking female speakers for their programs. "When a woman as good as a man may be secured," she noted, "the woman should be engaged."[22] She advised members to carefully monitor communications from other organizations "on which women are not represented, or not represented sufficiently." When members discovered that women had been overlooked, Kingsbury advised them to write personal letters "calling attention to the situation and asking that it be remedied."[23] Kathryn McHale was even more direct. Speaking to members of the South Atlantic Region after a presentation on Greek history, she said, "I am concerned with women's power, whether in Macedonian history or in American history."[24]

Beginning in the 1930s the Association actively promoted women for appointments to commissions, boards, government service, and university boards of trustees. The board encouraged each branch to "seek out, endorse, and actively support *highly qualified* women for public office."[25] Urging AAUW members to run for office, McHale said that next to securing favorable legislation, "one of the very best things that AAUW can do . . . is to get capable and courageous women on our school boards of education."[26] The branches often worked with the LWV and other women's organizations to urge women in their communities to assume public leadership roles. The Durham, North Carolina, branch, for example, played an important role in getting two representatives appointed to the local Citizens' Council of Public Affairs, a group that lobbied for various community groups to be included in the Community Fund budget and took part in an array of state safety campaigns and other projects.[27]

AAUW's intent, however, was not simply to place more women in office but to prove that women were capable of public service. McHale cautioned, "Just any woman in a position is not our goal. She must be the right person—one who has the ability to express herself and is not intimidated by a group of men, one who knows her work." AAUW standards for qualified women reflected the organization's commitment to high educational and cultural standards. McHale described women qualified for public office as having an "understanding and appreciation of the importance of schools and libraries in the cultural development of communities."[28]

No episode more strongly rallied AAUW members in their efforts to achieve recognition for qualified women than the fight that followed the appointment of a man to succeed Mary Woolley as president of Mount Holyoke.[29] The bitter debate that occurred in 1934–1935 over Woolley's successor highlighted questions of women's leadership and the recognition of women's achievement in the public sphere. Many women saw the Mount Holyoke trustees' appointment of a man to succeed Woolley as a direct attack on women's achievements. In April 1935 Kathryn McHale told Woolley, "The Association would regret very much losing any of the gains it had made in the recognition of women if the presidential tradition of Mount Holyoke were broken." Woolley replied, "It would be impossible to overemphasize my feeling with regard to the importance of having a woman as my successor."[30]

Joining the campaign to force the trustees to reconsider their action were many women who had been feminists and activists since before World War I, including Mount Holyoke alumnae and such prominent women as Frances Perkins and Carrie Chapman Catt. McHale and AAUW staff associate Esther Brunauer initiated an unofficial campaign within the Association. None of the women could accept the trustees' claim that there were no women qualified to serve as college president. "It may be true that there are today few women with long experience as college executives,"

Brunauer wrote, "but men college presidents are not always obtained by transferring successful executives from one institution to another. Regardless of sex, there is almost always some uncertainty as to how a new president will develop, and I submit that the proportion of successful presidents among the women heads of colleges is very high. A scarcity of already successful women college presidents for the filling of the Mount Holyoke vacancy does not seem to be a valid reason for turning away from women entirely."[31]

The Mount Holyoke controversy also highlighted the contention of many feminists that women possessed unique and special qualities. These feminists had come of age during a period of intense women's activity and identified strongly with women's organizations and social networks. For them, the women's colleges represented an important part of a women's culture, nourishing women's activism, feminism, and ambition. Many women, including Kathryn McHale, took the trustees' act as a personal insult to their own accomplishments and to the contribution women could make to society. McHale wrote, "Women have a creative contribution to make to women's education which is distinctive. They hold a social sector peculiarly their own, they are conservators and adjustors of life and in the acts of civilization their cultural role is superior."[32]

But the controversy did more than bring to public attention concerns about women's achievements and recognition; it also exposed an aspect of feminism between the wars that often remained unspoken. The question of Mary Woolley's personal life, particularly her relationship with Mount Holyoke English professor Jeanette Marks, lay not far beneath the surface of the controversy. Woolley had lived with Marks for many years, and speculation about their relationship had fueled quiet opposition to Woolley, especially toward the end of her tenure as college president. McHale was well aware of the intimacy between Woolley and Marks and felt that innuendo had influenced the trustees' decision.[33]

Perhaps even more important, the trustees' criticism of Woolley was symptomatic of a deep mistrust of the very women's culture in which women sought each other's allegiance, defended one other's potential, and which drew them into women's organizations. This mistrust was apparent in the *Boston Globe*'s assertion that a male college president would be "a fine tonic for the spinster management of Mt. Holyoke." McHale sharply criticized that statement, proclaiming, "The time has come for a crusade by women and for women."[34] Defending women's right to live as they choose, she asserted, "The principle of equality must not be confused with identity." Esther Brunauer also voiced her support of this aspect of feminism. In a letter to Jeanette Marks, she wrote, "It makes one ashamed of one's fellow human beings, to think that men of substance could have such small minds and such small souls and could be so vindictive."[35] Aware that the question of sexual orientation lay not far below the surface of the controversy, Brunauer tried to overcome the fears of the trustees. Writing to Mount Holyoke dean Edgar Furness, she insisted that her advocacy of Woolley "does not come from personal frustration or professional disappointment, for I have been exceptionally fortunate in an educational experience undisturbed by discrimination on a sex basis and a satisfying professional life accompanied by the happiest kind of relationships as a wife and mother."[36]

Despite the arguments raised, the Mount Holyoke trustees held firm in their position and refused to reconsider their presidential choice. By the end of 1936, when it became clear that outside pressure was having little effect on the board of trustees, McHale proposed that AAUW shift gears and begin work to ensure that the incident would not be repeated. Because the trustees had argued that they could not locate a qualified woman for the office, McHale suggested that AAUW begin to "keep names of fine women, suitable for academic posts, a little more before the public."[37] Meta Glass, who succeeded Woolley as Association president, similarly asserted, "My own way of capitalizing this regrettable happening for the future security of professional women would be to bolster and make known the work of capable women . . . to safeguard with good arguments and fine material [against] its occurrence again."[38]

AAUW women in the 1930s frequently pursued individual or professional career paths that were unusual for women even during the Depression. They were careful to protect their achievements and hoped to encourage younger women to follow their lead. The respect of the public and leading male educators and policy makers therefore loomed as vital to the success of AAUW aims. As the Association grew in size and scope, however, internal conflicts arose over the meaning of equality. In particular, opinion differed over how far the Association should go in expanding its legislative agenda and how broadly the organization's educational mission should be conceived.

The Association's 1935 convention theme, "The Role of Women as Makers of Social History," seemed to condone a broad interpretation of AAUW's mission. Inspired by New Deal openings in public policy, AAUW members led forays into consumer protection and social welfare measures. Asserting the special abilities and role of educated women in shaping public discourse and in leading social reform, AAUW women began to address the widespread social and economic problems of the Depression through public action. The Durham, North Carolina, branch, for example, helped establish the city's juvenile court, the Minneapolis branch studied the problems of public relief "preparatory to proposed legislation," and another Minnesota branch secured an "effective milk ordinance."[39] In 1935, the convention approved a resolution committing the organization to a broad program of support for public health and welfare legislation—and a call to decriminalize dispension of contraceptive devices by qualified physicians.

A birth control movement had been simmering since early in the century. That movement, along with changes in women's lives, particularly in education and employment, influenced a shift in public opinion on the question of contraception. By mid-decade, according to a Gallup poll, almost two-thirds of Americans favored the teaching and practice of birth control.[40] Although Margaret Sanger's Birth Control League was still considered a radical group, women in other groups began to debate the issue. Women increasingly questioned the legal restrictions on dispensing contraceptives and information about them. Seeing the issue as one of public health, many women began to advocate for increased access to contraceptives.[41]

In 1935, Louise Taylor-Jones, a member of the Washington, D.C., AAUW branch and former president of the Medical Women's National Association, brought before the AAUW Committee on Legislation a resolution calling for repeal of the criminal code that prohibited physicians from dispensing information on contraception. The resolution, "Item 8" of the legislative program, was opposed by only two board members from the Upper Midwest, who expected resistance from their largely Catholic branches. Kathryn McHale also had reservations about Item 8 but did not try to block the committee vote. The committee took its program to the 1935 convention and invited the Birth Control League to display information there. The entire legislative program passed, apparently without comment.[42]

Shortly after the convention, Kathryn McHale began receiving letters from outraged members who opposed contraception and considered Item 8 far outside the Association's educational mission. Sister M. Madeleva of St. Mary's College at Notre Dame wrote that her institution could not be associated with the "racket of contraseptics [sic]."[43] Mother M. Angelique, dean of Our Lady of the Lake College in San Antonio, Texas, wrote, "Certainly a very large number of the AAUW members, including myself, are convinced that, morally speaking, the furthering of knowledge of birth control by artificial methods will be most devastating." She based her argument not only on church doctrine but also on her belief that "birth control by contraceptive methods" was "detrimental both physically and mentally" to women. The trump card in her opposition to birth control was rooted in her own version of feminism. The issue, she said, "is one which stands most in need of our strongest womanly support." She added, "We are justly disgusted with pagan custom by which banqueters disgorged themselves in order that they might regale their appetites again. Birth control by contraceptive methods is certainly an infinitely deeper degradation."[44]

No one feared the repercussions of the birth control issue more than Kathryn McHale. Not only did she personally oppose birth control, but she was convinced that the issue could destroy the Association. "It is amazing to me," she told Northwest Central regional director Georgette Waters (one of the two Legislative Committee members who opposed Item 8), "to find some members in the Association quite complacent over the passage of this item." McHale confided to Waters, "There are several members who are greatly upset and we are in the latter group, I believe."[45]

McHale's quiet campaign revealed the extent of her influence among the members and her pragmatic approach to managing differences among them. She lobbied heavily with influential members of the board to convince them to reconsider—and defeat—the issue at the next convention. In addition, she urged women who were considering withdrawing their membership to stay in the Association, stressing the "tactical advantage" to fighting the issue from within and voting it down at the next convention.[46] The Association's legislative program, she argued, "does not constitute a permanent declaration of principle."[47]

McHale succeeded in convincing several board members and staff associates that the birth control program threatened the very life of AAUW. Association president Meta Glass supported McHale's quiet efforts to keep Catholic members in the Association and added her own voice to the general director's campaign. Looking to McHale for guidance, she asked if it would be wise for her to let Sister Thomas Aquinas know that she felt the Catholic member institutions should work more actively to get Item 8 rescinded. She assured McHale that other members stood ready to support them in their campaign "just to avoid having on our legislative program an item that threatens to split the Association."[48]

Other staff members shared McHale's concern that Item 8 would divide the Association. Ruth Tyron, editor of the Association's journal, feared that any publicity suggesting that AAUW supported birth control would seriously hurt the Association. In response, the Legislative Committee issued a statement to clarify the "misunderstanding" that AAUW advocated birth control. The As-

sociation, the committee wrote, "does not advocate birth control
. . . it has simply voted to support a measure to remove the restrictions of the criminal code which hamper physicians in this respect." Tyron advised the Legislative Committee to avoid speaking
to the press altogether. "There is no misunderstanding to be
cleared up as far as the Catholics are concerned," she said. "They
oppose exactly the legislation which we have endorsed."[49]

The controversy raged most strongly in the Upper Midwest Region, where Catholic bishops had recently launched a campaign
against birth control and against organizations that promoted contraception.[50] After traveling extensively through the Northwest
Central Region and discussing the issue of birth control with
AAUW members, Georgette Waters told Meta Glass, "Our Catholic members must, so long as their church forbids this practice, be
opposed to this part of our program." Waters feared antagonizing
so many members and warned Glass that the Association "should
keep hands off matters of religion." Although Waters personally
favored birth control, she felt it would be "a grave mistake to include it in our legislative program."[51] She acknowledged that although many branches endorsed "the principles for which Item 8
stands . . . we made a mistake using the word, 'contraceptive.' "[52]
Northwest Central regional vice president Clara Painter also worried about the ramifications of endorsement of Item 8 although she
personally favored birth control. "I cannot see how anyone who
looks at it [Item 8] solely from the point of view of the welfare and
growth of our Association," Painter said, "can fail to wish to see
it removed." Convinced that the Association should confine its
program to educational concerns, she added, "I do not wish to see
it interfere with the more important work of our AAUW."[53]

Members who supported Item 8 strenuously objected to any suggestion that it be dropped from the legislative program at the next
convention. The Iowa Division went on record in support of the
measure, arguing that other parts of the legislative program, particularly the items promoting maternal and infant health, child welfare, the promotion of general health, and disease prevention,
"could not be adopted with the intellectual approach worthy of

college women without the adoption of Item 8."[54] Mabel Merwin, director of the North Pacific Section, told McHale, "My own feeling is that we should stand pat. I regret loss of members, but I think that a minority has no right to dictate to a majority." Merwin added, "No Catholic woman need avail herself of the opportunity offered by the passage of such a law, and she has no right to make it impossible for others to do so."[55] Merwin advised McHale to inform those who objected to Item 8 that they had the "privilege" of withholding support but they should not "work against legislation to which the Association was committed nationally." In other words, they could simply ignore the item.

Other members called on the Association to stand on principle. Getting to the heart of the controversy, Minneapolis branch president Sally Spensley Michner contended that the Association had "adopted a principle in regard to legalizing the dispensing of information by physicians on contraception." To remove such information from its legal classification as "obscene," she argued, was consistent "with our traditional attitude toward scientific information."[56]

The fundamental issue raised by Item 8 was whether AAUW's focus on education would be interpreted in broad or narrow terms. Cedar Falls, Iowa, branch president Bess Faxau articulated the dilemma well when she wrote that to stave off the loss of Catholic members, the Association would have to stay away from "any mention of maternal and infant welfare . . . youth, juvenile delinquency etc. etc." The Association could not take a stand in favor of these measures, she said, "without the support of Item 8."[57] Faxau noted that her branch might be willing to "see legislation approved by AAUW confined to educational matters" but added, "I am confident that the branch is not willing to close its eyes to the fundamentals in considering legislation for social welfare." She argued that AAUW's willingness to fight for the right of physicians to dispense birth control information might "pave the way for Catholic women to achieve the freedom of their convictions in this matter."[58] She pointed to other national women's organizations, including the General Federation of Women's Clubs and the Business and Professional Women's Association, that had taken similar stands.[59]

Despite the arguments of those who supported Item 8, the board voted to drop the measure from the 1937–1939 legislative program. Swayed by McHale's argument that the organization would be split if Item 8 remained on the program, the board decided that "retaining the item was not important enough to risk division."[60] In the end, relatively few women left the Association because of the Item 8 controversy, and most of the Catholic institutions maintained their memberships.[61]

Ironically, the decision to drop Item 8 proved divisive, in its own way. During a bitter discussion among board members, the Legislative Committee argued that the Association could not "set up a social studies program which does not include a consideration of social legislation such as that described by this legislative item." Others argued that withdrawing the item would "cause resentment among the Protestant members" and make it appear that the board had been pressured by a Catholic lobby. But when asked "whether retaining the item was important enough to risk division," the majority opted for caution.[62] The controversy did take its toll; immediately after the board voted the entire Legislative Committee resigned.[63]

Neither AAUW nor women's groups generally were completely unified in their definition of feminism or their embrace of women's issues. Specific issues such as promoting women for public office, opposing discrimination against married women in employment, and including women in jury service united strong coalitions among women's groups, but other issues such as supporting the ERA, legalizing contraception, and the debate over Mary Woolley's successor divided them. If AAUW members disagreed about specific points in the Association's legislative program, they could all take pride in the organization's fellowship program, its support for equity in women's education, and the leadership they displayed in community affairs.

Chapter 3

WOMEN AS

WORLD CITIZENS

During the 1930s, women's organizations supported different definitions of feminism and strategies for women's advancement, but they were united in the arena of the international peace movement. International cooperation, disarmament, and opposition to war were the subjects of many of their programs.[1] Cooperating with Carrie Chapman Catt's National Committee on the Cause and Cure of War, AAUW charted its own international program during the 1920s focusing on education, research, and the role of women in international negotiations. During the 1930s, the Association's International Relations Program concentrated increasingly on protecting the status of women in international law, defending European women against increasing attacks in academic institutions, and assisting university women who became refugees in wartorn Europe. In addition, the International Relations Program exerted a critical influence on other Association programs.

The AAUW focused considerable energy during the early 1930s on the question of women's status in international law. Allying with other national women's organizations, AAUW lobbied vigorously for amendments to the Cable Act that would enable women to determine their own citizenship regardless of marital status or their husband's citizenship.[2]

If AAUW's position on international citizenship reflected the belief of its members in simple equality with men, its advocacy of women's representation on international commissions and boards, reflected a belief in women's unique sensibilities. The Association argued that women had a special interest in international peace and a capacity for cooperation and negotiation that would assist international organizations. In 1932 President Herbert Hoover appointed AAUW International Relations Committee chair Mary Woolley as the only woman at the Conference for the Reduction and Limitation of Armaments in Geneva.[3] Although columnist Will Rogers called her "the outstanding novelty" of the conference, Woolley's presence set an important precedent for women's representation at international gatherings.[4] Upon returning from a 1935 meeting of the NCCCW, Woolley assured Association members that they had a special "role in shaping public opinion toward peace."[5] She denounced "the old argument that women should have no voice in government because they could not bear arms to defend it," proclaiming instead that women's "united voices will make for peace."[6]

Under the guidance of Woolley and Virginia Gildersleeve, AAUW's International Relations Committee developed one of the Association's strongest and most popular programs. AAUW approached international relations with the same liberal faith in rational debate, expert leadership, and reward by merit that characterized its approach to the New Deal. More than 100 AAUW representatives regularly attended NCCCW conferences and played a major role in that body's policy making. AAUW branches sponsored study groups on international cooperation and circulated petitions calling for disarmament and the cooperation of all nations in the peace effort. Topics such as "The New Deal: National Isolation or World Cooperation," typified branch programs.[7] AAUW published books geared toward "building international attitudes in children" and urged local libraries to stock them.[8]

Also of concern to AAUW women in the late 1930s were the increasing attacks on the professional status and, indeed, the lives of European university women. Immediately after Adolph Hitler's rise to power in Germany in 1933, International Relations Committee staff associate Esther Brunauer began to warn American women of the dangerous developments in Europe. The threat of totalitarianism and the appeal to mob psychology, she argued, threatened the practices that formed the fundamental beliefs of AAUW women: reasoned discourse, informed citizenship, and intellectual freedom. After a visit to Germany in the early 1930s, Brunauer warned that Hitler's Nazi Party "set aside as of no value many aspects of modern culture which seem to us of greatest importance."[9]

The threat to women's academic freedom in Germany also directly threatened the political and social gains women had achieved in that country. German universities had long been models of high-quality education. In fact, many of the Association's early members had studied in Germany when opportunities for higher education were closed to women in the United States. By 1933, however, European scholars were "wandering around the world . . . eking out a living as best they can, because their opinions did not conform with the official doctrine."[10] When the German Federation of University Women expelled all non-Aryans—ordered by the government to do so or disband—the AAUW board appointed a special committee made up of Meta Glass, Virginia Gildersleeve, and Mary Woolley to "protest the suppression of intellectual freedom that is rapidly passing over European countries."[11]

Reflecting AAUW's approach to problem solving, the committee was instructed, first, to politely urge the German Federation of University Women to reconsider its action. Next, it was instructed to study the situation and urge the IFUW to collect information on "the feminist activities within [its] respective countries, with special emphasis on the achievements of women of university rank." Finally, the committee was asked to look for opportunities for teacher exchanges (including elementary and nursery teachers) and research possibilities and to develop a plan to aid displaced German women scholars.[12]

Unable to stem the tide of repression abroad, American women in the late 1930s and the war years threw themselves into refugee relief work. AAUW members identified strongly with displaced professional women and eagerly raised money to sponsor individual women and their families. In 1940 the Executive Committee declared that aid to university women and their children was "an urgent and immediate task" of the Association. By the end of that year AAUW women had raised almost $10,000 for refugee aid and by 1942 the Association had raised more than $27,000 for the University Women's War Relief Fund.[13] The Santa Monica branch proudly reported that members skipped their vacations in order to raise refugee aid. "It has meant something basic to the community to have this leadership by university women in this critical period," wrote the branch chair, "[and] it has meant much to the Branch to constructively channel the emotion we all feel."[14] The Asheville, North Carolina, branch raised more than $2000 for European university women by selling used clothing at a "Refugee Shop," and the Memphis branch raised $125.[15] Within weeks of the board's call for members to individually sponsor refugee children, it received applications from more than two thousand volunteers.[16] In a memo to branch presidents, Margaret Morriss assured them it was "not necessary to have great wealth" to sponsor a refugee child, but one's means must be sufficient . . . that another person can be supported over a long period of time."[17] AAUW women eagerly committed themselves for the duration.

AAUW separated itself from other prominent women's groups during the late 1930s by renouncing, for the first time, a strictly pacifist position. Events in Europe during the late 1930s, and calls to aid Britain in particular, divided the American peace movement.[18] As tensions mounted in Europe, other prominent women's organizations, such as the Women's International League for Peace and Freedom, continued to advocate strongly for maintaining U.S. neutrality in Europe. Esther Brunauer, on the other hand, urged the AAUW to modify its commitment to neutrality. AAUW withdrew from the National Council for Prevention of War at the end of 1938 because of the council's "mandatory neutrality stand."[19] By early 1939 Brunauer convinced the Association of the need to lobby U.S. senators to vote in favor of "cash and carry" and an embargo in the event of war in Europe.[20] Her renouncement of neutrality was mirrored by the position of the IFUW and British university women in particular. The Association supported legislation permitting an embargo on war supplies to Japan, and in June 1940 it declared general support for the repeal of the 1935 Neutrality Act.[21] Brunauer called the vote on the Neutrality Act "thrilling" and declared that women had made a real contribution to making "resistance to totalitarian aggression effective."[22] McHale, too, supported an end to neutrality. Speaking of Mary Woolley, who maintained her opposition to the war, McHale said, "I consider her one of the most sincere and spiritual characters I have ever known but as events proved, all pacifists have too long done wishful thinking."[23]

Brunauer and McHale parted company with many old allies over the question of neutrality. At least three board members resigned after the vote on the Neutrality Act. Their feelings were summarized by Harriet Connor Brown, AAUW's delegate to the NCCCW, who wrote Brunauer a scathing letter suggesting that "you younger women study the Transactions of the Women's Congress at the Hague in 1915." Brown favored neutral and continuous mediation in which no party would be labeled the victor. "It is little short of tragic," she wrote, "that you are not better informed in regard to the efforts of women in the first World-War [*sic*] to stop hostilities, that you are perhaps too young to remember clearly that statesmanlike proposal of the women of many nations failed because the Wilson Administration refused to take the initiative which the other governments of the world were not only willing, but even eager, it should take."[24]

Despite the protests of Brown and other older-generation AAUW members, the Association membership by and large appeared to support Brunauer and McHale. Indeed, after the United States entered the war, the voices of opposition within the Association, as in other women's groups, grew quiet. AAUW boasted that it had been the first national women's organization to advocate aid to "those countries fighting for human rights, even at the risk of war," and the *New York Times* credited AAUW with setting a precedent "for other more timorous groups of women."[25]

After the attack on Pearl Harbor, the Association devoted its full energies toward the war effort. Motivated by patriotic fervor and a desire to demonstrate women's leadership abilities during a time of crisis, AAUW urged women to become involved in community education, civil defense, and refugee aid. "It is often said that women in crises retreat," observed Kathryn McHale. AAUW to the contrary, she proudly noted, "engages in an all out effort to serve our country."[26] Underlying the Association's war efforts was a conviction that women could—and should—take an equal role in national defense. In 1942, McHale told AAUW members that their Association "represents the intellectual women, the educated women, the woman leaders of America. We must realize our importance in the Battle of Mankind." The issue, she said, was "how to give ourselves as a trained group, as an organization obligated to serve where our training will do most good."[27] Margaret Morriss asked branches to suspend their usual calendars and focus exclusively on the war effort.[28] AAUW, along with other national organizations, suspended national meetings during the war, and many state and local gatherings ceased. Women in communities throughout the nation rationed gasoline, limited phone calls, and developed new recipes necessitated by wartime shortages in such foods as sugar and butter. The Durham, North Carolina, branch, for example, informed members of meetings by postcard rather than phone calls. Many branches and state divisions cut back on travel and urged members to "drive with others" if they had to attend meetings.[29]

After Pearl Harbor women began to take advantage of new opportunities to use their professional training. Women confidently expected not only that their expertise would aid in the national crisis but that their work would prove women capable of leadership and deserving of equity in public life. AAUW women particularly focused on new opportunities opening up for women in military service. More than 350,000 women served in the armed forces during the war. AAUW, the BPW, and other women's groups lobbied extensively for commissions for women in the armed forces and for equal benefits including medical care and retirement.[30] Virginia Gildersleeve and her longtime companion, Elizabeth Reynard, helped to found the Navy's auxiliary corps, the WAVES (Women Accepted for Volunteer Emergency Service), and board members Helen Dwight Reid and Esther Brunauer served on the national board of the Women's Army Corps (WAC).[31]

During the war AAUW women began to chart a new course in their search for equality. Again parting company with many other feminists, AAUW advocated military service for women. Only the BPW actively joined AAUW in this call. Other women's organizations, like the WTUL, supported the idea in principle but did not pursue the issue.[32] Few shared AAUW's forthright advocacy of a military commitment for women. Lucy Somerville Howorth, a member of the AAUW Committee on the Economic and Legal Status of Women, announced, "I believe that women should be drafted now for the armed forces of the U.S.A." Howorth advocated drafting women for practical reasons as well as principle: "Each day the war lasts the cleavage between those who have served and sacrificed and those who have not grows deeper," she observed, "and if the men, particularly overseas men, begin to believe that the women are letting them down, there will be a great bitterness in the future."[33] Another committee member, Sarah Hughes, observed, "The benefits of victory in this war will be the same for men and women. The obligations to their country should be the same."[34] In fact, when the question of a National Service Act arose in 1944, the Association declared it would support a national draft only if it included women. Staff associate Frances Speek said, "As the AAUW has always worked for equal recognition of women's abilities, so it is now appropriate for it to work for women's required service to their country."[35]

Lucy Somerville Howorth represented a new generation of AAUW women who came into prominence during World War II. The daughter of Nellie Nugent Somerville, Mississippi's first woman legislator (who served from 1924 until 1928), Lucy grew up in a household that advocated women's participation in public life. She graduated from Randolph-Macon Women's College in 1916 and went on to Columbia for graduate work. Lucy's ambition was to study law, but she soon discovered that none of the top law schools would admit women. Hence, she returned to Mississippi where she received her bachelor of law degree magna cum laude from the University of Mississippi. As the only female lawyer in Jackson, she formed a joint law firm with her husband, fellow law student Joseph Marion Howorth. During the 1920s her legal work included industrial research for the National Board of the YWCA and a stint as U.S. commissioner for the Southern Judicial District of Mississippi. In 1931 she followed her mother into the state legislature.[36]

By the end of the decade, Howorth had gained a national reputation as a feminist and a jurist. She became active in AAUW during World War II, serving as a member of several national committees and chairing the CELSW from 1947 to 1951. During the war she pressed for equity for women in military service. She encouraged women to use their skills for the war effort and at the same time pushed government officials to recognize women's potential contribution and to afford them equal status with men in the civil defense as well as military service. After the war she served as the principal attorney of the Veterans Appeals Board and the only woman to serve as General Counsel to the War Claims Commission. Howorth remained an influential member of the AAUW board during the 1950s and, as a southerner, played an important role in guiding the Association toward racial integration.[37]

Within a week of Pearl Harbor, President Roosevelt, acting under a War Powers Act, authorized scores of special wartime agencies to regulate domestic, civilian life. AAUW and other women's groups immediately moved to ensure women's participation in these efforts. Reflecting the belief of many AAUW women, staff member Elizabeth Fuller Jackson told a Durham, North Carolina, member, "Upon no other group of American women is the burden of responsibility so great as it is upon us who have been specially privileged in education."[38] AAUW instituted a system of registration within its own ranks to create rosters of women it could recommend for defense councils and civilian leadership. The registration effort was so impressive that in 1941, when New York's Mayor Fiorello La Guardia was appointed Director of the Office of Civilian Defense, he asked to use the registration cards as a model and recruited Esther Brunauer to the Office of Civilian Defense "to get things going."[39]

Despite its general support for the war effort, AAUW drew back from federal policies that explicitly threatened equal rights. Association president Helen White wrote to McHale of her concern that women's dormitories, so recently won on some campuses, were summarily being taken over by the Army to house soldiers. "We should be watching the situation," she wrote, "and remind administrators of the increasing importance of women's training at the present time."[40]

AAUW also objected to a wartime proposal that would make it mandatory for married couples to file joint income tax returns. The tax appeared to pit patriotism against the right of women to control their own earnings. According to Frances Speek, secretary of the CELSW, mandatory joint returns would negate a married woman's separate identity and "right to property and earnings under her own name and control."[41] Testifying before a congressional committee, Dorothy Kenyon articulated AAUW's position on taxation and mandatory joint returns, saying: "In so far as taxation is a necessary part of the war effort we of the AAUW are 100 percent for it. Taxation holds no terrors for us. . . . But it is precisely because the tax is for freedom and not for slavery that we voice our objections today."[42]

During World War II, AAUW women made every effort to demonstrate their capacity for community leadership and public service. Helen White, the Association president during the war years, was convinced, as were many women of her generation, that hard work and high standards would ultimately earn them recognition and respect. Born in New Haven, Connecticut, in 1896, White was one of three literary sisters. After receiving a B.A. from Radcliffe College in 1916 and a master's degree the following year, she accepted a teaching appointment at the University of Wisconsin. By 1924 she had completed her Ph.D. in English, and in 1936 she became the first woman appointed full professor at the University of Wisconsin. White was also the first woman to lead the university's Teacher's Union and the first woman president of the University Club. In 1956 White achieved yet another milestone when she was elected the first woman president of the American Association of University Professors. One of the few women to receive a Guggenheim Fellowship, she received many honors for her scholarly work on William Blake, British literature, and sixteenth- and seventeenth-century Catholic history, as well as for several novels that she wrote. White loved to read Agatha Christie mysteries and to travel. She joined AAUW during the mid-1930s and shortly thereafter became a member of the national Fellowship Funds Committee. As a member and later as president of AAUW, she identified strongly with the organization as a professional woman, but she also recognized that many college graduates became housewives. Of them she commented, "Civilization survives because of the little people."[43]

Like many other American women, White trusted that women's professional qualifications plus their visible wartime contributions would ensure them a prominent place in the public arena after the war. AAUW, along with the BPW, National Council of Negro Women (NCNW), YWCA, LVW, and WTUL, actively pressed federal officials to acknowledge women's contributions and to realize the promise of equity in the process of reconversion.[44] In 1944 AAUW, BPW, and other women's groups held a White House Conference on Women in Policy-Making at which speakers advocated for the appointment of women to public positions both nationally and internationally. They urged women to run for elective offices and supported the appointment of women to policy-making boards and commissions.[45]

Indeed, AAUW women were well represented both in Washington and at postwar international conferences. A contingent of AAUW women acted as representives of nongovernmental agencies at the San Francisco conference founding the United Nations (UN) in

1946, and AAUW continued to support UN and UNESCO activities throughout the postwar years.

By the time the war ended, many of the hostilities among women's organizations had begun to subside, particularly those centered around the ERA. The collective efforts of these groups in support of the war effort combined with the coming of age of a generation of women relatively free from the bitterness of ERA conflicts lessened some of the traditional mistrust toward groups that supported the ERA. In this more congenial atmosphere women's groups reconsidered their position on the amendment. Improvements in workplace conditions for women during the war and the institution of New Deal protections for all industrial workers made the ERA's threat to legislation protecting women in the workforce appear less susbstantial. In addition, many women, having devoted their energies to the war effort, felt the time had come for a recognition of equality and an end to discrimination. Finally, women's work for the United Nations provided an international context for a reconsideration of the ERA. The new UN, in which many women put considerable hope and energy, adopted provisions mandating human rights and equality not unlike the terms of the ERA. Many women began to feel that they could not honestly work for equality in the international arena if their own nation refused to grant women equal rights. By the late 1940s, a number of national women's organizations, including the National Federation of Women's Clubs and the BPW, reversed their opposition and endorsed the amendment.[46]

Although AAUW maintained its official opposition to the ERA through the postwar period, pressure from women within the Association began to force a rethinking of the issue. AAUW women became increasingly vocal in expressing views that conflicted with the official position. Sarah Hughes, for example, upon being invited to chair the CELSW in 1943, told Kathryn McHale, "While I have not concerned myself about the Amendment, because I felt that it was of such slight importance and had no chance of passing, I am in favor of it in principle, and have never opposed it." McHale assured Hughes that the Association was also in favor of the principle of equality for women but opposed the amendment "as a *method* of obtaining equality."[47] Hughes's interest in women's issues clearly did not center on the ERA, and she agreed to take on the committee chair.

Sarah Hughes was a dominating force on the CELSW during the war years. Born Sarah Tilghman in Baltimore in 1896, she graduated from Goucher College and earned a law degree from George Washington University. While in law school she met Texas native George Hughes, and in 1922 they married and moved to Dallas. Finding employment was more difficult than Hughes anticipated. After being turned down by "every law firm in Dallas," she opened her own law practice. This experience persuaded her to become a "staunch women's rights activist," and eight years later she was elected to the Texas legislature. In the legislature Hughes promoted women's interests, authoring, for example, the bill that allowed Texas women to serve on juries. She became the state's first female district judge, a post to which she was reelected six times. While serving as chair of the CELSW, Hughes continued to pursue her political career. In 1946 she made an unsuccessful bid for Congress, and in 1958 she sought a seat on the Texas Supreme Court. Surprised at the amount of resistance she encountered in her bids for public office, Hughes commented, "People were willing to vote for me for judge because they thought that I would be fair. But they were not willing to vote for me in a place where I could change the laws."[48] Hughes continued to be active in AAUW, serving as a regional vice president and as chair of the CELSW from 1943 to 1947, and in the BPW, where she was elected national president in 1950. Hughes also became a well-known figure in the Democratic Party. She held the distinction of having been nominated for vice president to serve with Adlai Stevenson in 1952, but she quickly withdrew her name from the race. Later, President John Kennedy named her to the federal bench, and she had the honor of swearing in Lyndon Johnson after Kennedy's assassination.

As head of the CELSW during the war, Hughes pushed for a broad program of women's rights. During her tenure on the committee, AAUW supported equal pay legislation, jury service for women, an end to discrimination against married women, and the appointment of women to public office. In 1944 Hughes represented AAUW at the White House Conference on Women in Policy-Making, where she promoted the use of women's talents and skills in public office and spearheaded the formation of state conferences on women in public policy.[49]

Hughes's position on the ERA ultimately brought her into conflict with an older generation of Association activists. Although both she and McHale downplayed the importance of the ERA, some board members worried that Hughes was using her office to oppose the Association's official position.[50] Board president Helen White warned her not to promote her private views to the general membership saying, "It was proper for you to express your disagreement in the board meeting, but I agree with those members who feel that it would be very unfortunate if you should appeal from the board, say to the convention." Putting aside her hesitations, however, White asked Hughes to serve a second term.[51] By 1947, Hughes apparently could no longer support the Association's opposition to the ERA and, after a "difficult discussion" at a board meeting, offered her resignation.[52]

Hughes was not alone in her frustration over AAUW's continued opposition to the ERA. Former CELSW member Dorothy Kenyon, saying it was "time to heal the breach between [sic] women in the United States," urged AAUW in 1946 to support a compromise amendment that would "not be construed to invalidate any existing or future laws or regulations which safeguard the health, safety, and welfare of women."[53] Lucy Howorth joined Hughes in urging AAUW to take a public stand in favor of the ERA. When the members were unable to come to a consensus on the issue, Hughes and Howorth suggested that the Association take no official stand at all rather than continue its opposition to the Amendment.[54]

Despite the efforts of Hughes and others to modify AAUW's position on the ERA, the Association clung to its opposition. Opponents continued to be convinced that women's special protections would be sacrificed while proponents argued that women now, more than ever, needed full and absolute equality. In 1946 AAUW joined with other traditional ERA opponents to form the National Committee on the Status of Women (originally the National Committee to Defeat the Un-Equal Rights Amendment). The committee supported the Women's Status Bill, which called for an end to discrimination on the basis of sex "except where reasonably justified by differences in physical structure or biological or social function."[55] Neither the ERA nor the Women's Status Bill succeeded in passing Congress, and AAUW continued to officially oppose the Amendment.

The breakdown of solid opposition to the ERA among women's organizations after the war suggests the beginning of a change in the nature of national women's organizations and in the women's culture that had characterized them since the late nineteenth century. One sign of this changing perspective came in 1946 when, in order to be more "modern," the CELSW changed its name to Committee on the Status of Women.[56] Whereas women of the older generation believed in women's special qualities and fundamental gender differences, women of the war generation saw fewer differences between men and women, particularly in their role in the public sphere. Those AAUW members, for example, who favored a draft for women no longer argued that women were different from men; instead they argued simply that women, like men, should be able to realize their individual potential unhampered by arbitrary barriers and discrimination. Indeed, women had successfully run businesses, public agencies, and defense committees during the war and they fully expected that their contributions, like those of men, would be acknowledged and rewarded by future opportunities. But the very fact that women had operated in a mixed-gender world during the war led them away from the separate woman-centered organizational orientation of the prewar years. Women would continue to gravitate toward women's organizations, but their orientation toward a woman-centered culture had been altered.

Part II

WOMEN'S CULTURE
AND THE CRISIS OF
AMERICAN LIBERALISM,
1945–1960

By most accounts, the women's movement died during
the 1950s. Described by some as "the doldrums" and
by others as an era in which the search for security
after two decades of depression and war led American
women to focus on family life to the exclusion of
public concerns, the 1950s appears to be a decade of
passivity and domesticity.[1] A closer examination of
women's organizations during the 1950s suggests the
need for a reevaluation of feminism's fate during that
decade. Women's organizations neither disappeared
nor remained silent about women's rights during the
cold war years. AAUW's membership, for example,
grew, its fellowship program expanded and it
established the AAUW Educational Foundation, and the
Committee on the Status of Women never stopped
pressing for equity in law, employment, and politics.

An exploration of AAUW activities during the 1950s
suggests not a declining interest in women's issues but
rather a transformation in the language, context, and

culture of liberal politics. In the postwar climate of cold war, conflict and confrontation—indeed, dissent generally—became difficult. Women's groups did not abandon hopes for equality, but they did adopt a universalistic language of consensus and withdrew from national political coalitions. The context for a discussion of feminism also changed during the 1950s as women faced a serious challenge to their educational and professional opportunities. Although the number of women in the workforce increased after World War II, many spaces in the nation's colleges and professional schools were reserved for returning (male) veterans. The traditional constituency for women's organizations—middle-class, educated, and professional women—found itself under siege as the popular culture insisted on an ever wider dichotomy between the public and the private spheres. Finally, the culture of women's organizations was transformed during the 1950s by a confrontation between liberal egalitarianism and racial prejudice. Women's groups historically nurtured a culture that spoke for universal equality but at the same time depended upon exclusive, homogeneous social networks. The postwar civil rights movement challenged that culture, and demands for integration precipitated a crisis of identity for liberal groups such as AAUW. The Association's path during the 1950s reflects the fate of mainstream feminism during a time when Americans generally were reevaluating their relationships to public institutions and individual security.

Chapter 4

RETREAT FROM CONFLICT

A climate of consensus and anticommunism shaped the postwar political context in which women's organizations and other liberal reform groups operated. The cold-war atmosphere led many liberal groups to fear association with organizations that might be deemed unpatriotic and to cautiously word their public statements in ways that would assure members and the public alike of their patriotism. AAUW women considered themselves informed citizens and patriots in the best American tradition of democracy. The Association traditionally defended academic freedom and free speech as issues of critical importance not only to women but to the very foundations of democratic society. However, its positions on women's rights, international cooperation, and educational reform placed the Association squarely in the camp of American liberal reform most vulnerable to cold-war attack. Women who had devoted their lives to organizations pursuing equality and recognition for women outside the domestic sphere found their loyalty in question.

Women's groups had never been immune from attacks on their loyalty and commitment to an American way of life. Antifeminists often saw women's groups as un-American, focusing particularly on their members' pursuit of professional lives and their prewar commitment to pacifism. Indeed, during the 1920s, women's groups as diverse as the NWP and the WILPF were linked to "international communism."[1] In 1939 Martin Dies's House Un-American Activities Committee (HUAC) attacked the AAUW "along with some of its prominent members," including Mary Woolley and Susan Kingsbury, as being subversive.[2] AAUW's response to the Dies Committee allegations reflected the Associations's strong feminist identity as well as its devotion to academic freedom. One board member said the committee was "a menace to democratic institutions and therefore a menace to the position of women in a democracy."[3] Others strongly protested the committee's investigations and defended the right of citizens to criticize government actions that they deemed threatening to basic freedoms. Association president Margaret Morriss declared, "I think the Dies Committee is more dangerous than the communists many times over, and that we are under obligation to protest."[4] In fact, few Board members hesitated to speak out publicly against the Dies Committee. Kathryn McHale announced, "This is the time for us to be courageous and active. . . . We are seeing in this country the beginnings of 'witch hunts,' book burnings, etc. AAUW cannot hesitate to act when convinced that the search for truth, freedom of thought and expression are in jeopardy."[5]

After World War II, however, the threat of Soviet expansion and nuclear war set an entirely different tone. HUAC once again took up the active pursuit of subversives within the American government, and voluntary organizations were again subjected to scrutiny by government bodies as well as private community groups. Government and private employers pressured employees to demonstrate their loyalty, and hundreds lost their jobs because of alleged subversive connections. According to one historian, "By early 1951 the Civil Service Commission had cleared over 3 million people, while over 2,000 had resigned and 212 had been dismissed for doubtful loyalty." Although "no espionage ring was uncovered," many lives were disrupted.[6]

While HUAC, along with the Senate's most vociferous anti-communist spokesman, Joseph McCarthy, uncovered few communists in government, their investigations and accusations created an atmosphere of fear and suspicion. Coming just as the Cold War divided the international scene between democracy and communism, McCarthyism created a devastating climate for political dissent at home. In 1950, over President Harry Truman's veto, Congress passed the McCarran Internal Security Act, which established the Subversive Activities Control Board to discourage Communists and Communist sympathizers from operating in the United States.[7]

Like that of the nation as a whole, the Association's response to postwar HUAC hearings was more ambivalent than prewar sentiments had been. In the context of an international cold war, few liberal organizations questioned the need for heightened concern over internal security and individual loyalty. At the same time, many liberals hoped to salvage a respect for individual liberty and the right to dissent. Ultimately, liberal organizations, including AAUW, found it almost impossible to reconcile these positions. As attacks on academics, intellectuals, and political dissidents increased during the early 1950s, the climate of political discourse radically shifted. Where before the war AAUW women felt themselves part of a tradition of political dissent committed to individual rights and women's opportunities, the cold-war era stifled dissent of any type, particularly when the dissenters were women who stepped out of the domestic sphere. The attacks on women's organizations revealed a deep-seated sense of insecurity within the political culture and gave voice to a strong antifeminist sentiment. Most liberals found McCarthy's tactics distasteful but accepted the presence of a pervasive threat to national security. Within this atmosphere, women's organizations found it necessary to fundamentally modify their approaches to feminism.

The most dramatic example of the shift in attitude toward political dissent was the career of AAUW general director Kathryn McHale. In 1950, after serving as the Association's central figure for two decades, McHale resigned to take a position as the first (and only) woman on the Subversive Activities Control Board (SACB). In one sense, service on the SACB fulfilled one of McHale's long-held ambitions—her desire to ensure women's representation on public boards and commissions. At the same time, the board McHale chose to join was one many of her colleagues considered inimical to the principle of academic freedom that the Association had upheld throughout her tenure as general director. In her work for the SACB McHale forswore feminism in favor of anticommunism. Under her direction the SACB conducted lengthy hearings on groups such as the Abraham Lincoln Brigade, which she condemned for left-wing activities.[8] In 1952 she defended the board's investigation of liberal organizations, arguing that "many legislative activities and principles can be found and one must be sure that innocent organizations are not indicted, when such exist; but those that stem from the parental organization that is accused of world domination stemming from foreign control must be parceled out."[9]

McHale's enthusiastic embrace of anticommunism was not shared by Helen Bragdon, her successor as AAUW general director. By early 1953, Bragdon had become increasingly alarmed at the strategy of what she called the "attacking groups," which not only supported government investigations but were also, as she put it, "acting from within." She warned board members Lucy Somerville Howorth and Susan Riley that right-wing groups were increasingly "representing themselves as belonging to some well-established organizations, like United Church Women" or AAUW itself.

Helen Bragdon's appointment as general director came during a period of intense conflict within AAUW. The McCarthy accusations combined with ongoing debate about race relations highlighted tensions within the organization. Bragdon faced the difficult tasks of healing these internal divisions and defending the Association from outside attack. During her tenure, from 1950 to 1959, she led the Association through those difficulties and managed to shape the AAUW into a financially sound women's organization.

Bragdon inherited a divided organization struggling to keep sight of its central mission of equity for women in education and public life. Much of Bragdon's time and energy were spent parrying attacks from the Right, defending individual rights, reasoned public discourse, and the right to dissent. She also had to balance forces within the Association, many of which were deeply critical of its national program.

The fate of AAUW staff associate Esther Caukin Brunauer dramatically and tragically highlighted the difficult situation AAUW faced as it tried to balance individual rights with national security concerns during the McCarthy Era. Brunauer, trained as a sociologist, devoted her professional career to AAUW and her intellectual energies to international cooperation and world peace. As a doctoral student at Stanford in 1926, she received the Association's Margaret E. Maltby Fellowship to complete her dissertation entitled "Peace Proposals of the Central Powers, 1914–18." The next year, degree in hand, she joined the AAUW staff as secretary of the International Relations Committee.[10]

Brunauer's work for AAUW focused primarily on the issues of peace and, later, refugee assistance. Her work, she said, gave her the opportunity to apply her training in history and politics to a project in adult education. She traveled to Europe every summer to pursue her research and ultimately published several articles on international cooperation and world peace in both German and English. During the 1930s, Brunauer, along with many American internationalists, became extremely alarmed at developments in Germany. She wrote and spoke widely on the subject, warning the American public against national socialism and the growing influence of Hitler's political party. She was most disturbed by the way political culture was being manipulated in Germany. She wrote, "If it could be done in Germany, it could be done in any other country. This mass movement simply set aside as of no value many aspects of modern culture which seem to us of greatest importance." The Nazi Party's manipulation of cultural symbols and mass emotion deeply disturbed Brunauer because it so directly contradicted her belief in the importance of education, rational debate, and informed citizenship.[12]

During the 1930s, Caukin combined her AAUW work with family life, marrying Hungarian born chemist Stephen Brunauer. Her work with the International Relations Committee took her to numerous national and international meetings, often as an organizer and occasionally as a speaker. During the World War II years, she became very active in refugee-relief work, shaping AAUW's program to assist European university women who were victims of discrimination and oppression. In 1944 she left AAUW to work for the State Department as assistant director of policy and liaison to the United Nations Educational, Scientific, and Cultural Organization (UNESCO). Four years later her husband became chief chemist for the Navy's Bureau of Ordinance.[12]

The postwar anti-Communist hysteria quickly shattered the Brunauers' careers. Although Stephen Brunauer had been given a loyalty clearance in 1949, he was suspended in 1951 as a security risk. The reason appeared to be that while visiting Hungary on official business after the war, he had contacted old friends whose politics were under suspicion. In March 1950, McCarthy included Esther Brunauer among those State Department employees he accused of being communists. In addition, McCarthy accused the AAUW of being a "front enterprise," citing in particular the Association's consumer program, which called for grade labeling of canned goods to enforce price controls. He later made additional accusations against Brunauer in an effort to tie her to international Communist connections.

In the charged cold-war climate, even unsubstantiated accusations often resulted in public condemnation and loss of employment. Although Brunauer agreed to testify before McCarthy's committee and was cleared of all charges, she was subsequently suspended from the State Department as a "security risk." Brunauer was forced to leave the work she loved and the AAUW to which she had devoted more than twenty years of her life. Stephen Brunauer ultimately secured a job in private industry, and Esther Brunauer eventually found work in the Library of Congress.

Esther Brunauer's reaction to the charges against her demonstrated the ambivalence with which American liberals viewed the McCarthy investigations. Neither Brunauer nor the AAUW women who defended her questioned the necessity of the government to conduct its investigations. Although Brunauer, like most liberals, disliked McCarthy's tactics, she shared the senator's assumption that American democracy was under serious threat from communism. Brunauer carefully answered every charge and elaborately attempted to prove that she "never became involved in the activities of fellow travelers, much less out and out communists." During the summer of 1948, when charges were first levied against her, Brunauer wrote to Kathryn McHale, "There is certainly nothing vindictive or arbitrary in the attitudes of the people who are carrying out this program, and I have the feeling that, as unpleasant as this situation is, it does provide an opportunity for straightening up the record and being protected in the future." Brunauer proceeded to document how her work was directly contrary to any Communist program. "The central theme and purpose of all my work," she wrote, "has been to develop sounder and broader understanding of international affairs, and . . . in so far as my work has had any concrete results, it has been through the increased support for participation of the United States in international organizations. It is certainly not my fault that the communists from time to time support some of the same policies that I have supported." Thinking back to criticisms she had received while working in AAUW, she noted, "As far as I can recall those charges relating to my political views were from people like Mary Beard who gave me far too much credit for the position that AAUW took in support of the Allies against the Nazis." Still, she said, "the very thought that anybody could consider me either disloyal to my country or so stupid as to fall for the communist line hurts a good deal."[13] Later she confided to McHale, "This is really an awfully hard experience to have to go through."[14]

The AAUW leadership rallied to Brunauer's defense—and to a defense of the Association as well. Kathryn McHale insisted that Brunauer's AAUW writings showed "not the slightest evidence of communist sympathies." On the contrary, "She consistently employed and encouraged an objective approach to international questions which is anathema to those with Communist leanings." Brunauer's approach, McHale said, was that "of the scholar, absolutely impartial and objective in evaluating all facts germane to an international problem." McHale also emphasized Brunauer's "personal and professional integrity, devotion to the public good, and loyalty to the government of the United States." McHale noted that during Brunauer's seventeen-year tenure at AAUW, "I had many opportunities to converse with her on the objectives of American foreign policy and our international program and thereby learned her philosophy of life and government. At no time did she express any opinions but that which would indicate that she was a true and loyal American citizen entitled to the respect of any God-fearing citizen. She is a conservative, liberal in thought, and believes strongly in the American form of government."[15] Helen Bragdon, in an extended defense of Brunauer, took great pains to differentiate between those who were accused of "disloyalty" and those who constituted a "security risk." The distinction, she said, hinged on the nature of one's associations. "Doubts as to loyalty," wrote Bragdon, "reflect directly on the individual," whereas doubts as to security "may be raised because of associations with persons who, it is thought, might wish to obtain secret information." Bragdon pointed out that although Brunauer was said to be a security risk, her AAUW work during the Hitler–Stalin pact was for programs "vehemently denounced by Communist sympathizers. Brunauer's whole record as an AAUW associate, Bragdon insisted, was that of "one whose first and deep concern was the preservation of American democracy."[16]

In addition to Brunauer, other AAUW leaders (and an unknown number of members) also came under attack during the McCarthy years. The Status of Women chair, Sarah Hughes, was the first person to appear before McCarthy's Senate subcommittee. Although she denied that she was a communist and eventually was cleared of the charge, the experience stripped her of any opportunity to pursue her political ambitions.[17] Kathryn McHale also came under attack. Her appointment to the SACB was delayed because of charges stemming from her defense of Brunauer and Hughes. There is also some suggestion that the investigation of McHale included charges that she was a lesbian.[18] Helen Bragdon, concerned about the consequences of the investigation, warned AAUW members that the loyalty probes threatened not only "individuals whom we know and in whom we have confidence" but also "the concepts of justice which have been the cornerstone of American democracy." Bragdon reminded AAUW women that they had a responsibility to "make a contribution to sane public opinion." She urged them not to shrink from the conflict but to follow the investigations and analyze HUAC 's "methods of inquiry, its objectives, and its effect on our public service."[19]

Despite Bragdon's plea for reason, some branches were split apart by the distrust and fear of the era. In the San Diego branch, for example, anti-communism combined with the integration issue to create an extremely bitter atmosphere. In another California branch, the atmosphere was so charged that branch leaders suspended all fellowship activities when some members "pointed the pink finger" at the family of one of the recipients. The Oshkosh, Wisconsin branch also experienced a long period of bitterness that put many of the liberal members on the defensive. Gretta A. Burchfield, the program chairman for the Kalamazoo, Michigan, branch, lamented the situation in her community: "I am increasingly disturbed," she wrote to Helen Bragdon, "over the tendency of branches and individuals in our organization to support the sniping and accusations directed toward very fine and able persons interested in world affairs. . . . We are having more and more accusations from members to the effect that we are bringing communists to speak to our groups. If it weren't so tragic, it would be hilariously funny because of the absurdity of the accusations." She saw the same thing happening in other community and church groups, but, she said, "it seems infinitely worse when AWU [*sic*] members will accept rumor for fact, innuendo for truth and accusations without documented evidence." She saw the investigations and their consequences as "an insidious menace to us, our organization and our institutions."[20]

Fear of ideas and suspicion of public figures challenged AAUW's self-image and educational mission. Association president Susan Riley said in 1951, "One of the disintegrating qualities of our time is fear. . . . Some of the fears . . . are wholesome: fears for our safety on traffic-clogged roads; for the protection of our children against disease, vulgarity, and crime; for the preservation of our country and our way of life . . . such fear breeds courage and teaches man how to survive in the presence of danger. Only when it paralyzes rather than stimulates, when it chills rather than warms the spirit, does it become an enemy."[21] Social Studies Committee chair, Ina Corinne Brown echoed Riley's warnings. In her report to the Association board she expressed concern that the Association's mission would be undermined by the members' "growing fear and distrust of one another." She pointed to the conflicts that had arisen in many branches involving "irresponsible name-calling and accusations, . . . people's taking sides against one another, the extreme right and the extreme left, capital and labor, this, that and the other group pulling in opposite directions."[22]

For AAUW women, the chilling effects of fear were most evident in intellectual and academic circles. AAUW women had long counted on a rational intellectual environment where women's achievements would be appreciated and rewarded. But in the cold-war era the atmosphere of fear and suspicion that infused so many academic centers threatened intellectual integrity, and the irrational tone of public debate threatened women's gains in professional life. Corinne Brown particularly feared that the "growing social disorganization" would result in "the lowering of standards, the giving up of the things that really matter."[23] Nancy Duke Lewis cautioned that the "fear of ideas" could directly affect women's educational opportunities. The academic fields in which women were most represented were the ones most threatened by the fear of free discussion of ideas. Schools responded to the cold-war fears, Lewis pointed out, by developing "an overconservative liberal arts program or letting [their liberal arts programs] go by the boards, with the emphasis on engineering, sciences and mathematics, as the safety of these subjects lies in their noncontroversial nature." Warning that "neutral education . . . could readily be used by a Hitler or a Stalin, as well as by a loyal American," Lewis pointed to the very concrete impact that anti-communist fear had already exerted on endowment sources, which had begun to emphasize technical programs and funded fewer and fewer programs in the liberal arts.[24] The consequences for women were clear.

Association president Susan Riley warned of the special danger to professional women in a cultural climate that emphasized conformity and mediocrity. As teachers and academics, they treasured rational discourse. "Faith and courage," Riley advised, "are needed to oppose the stultifying fears of our day." In the current climate, she cautioned, "the untutored and inexperienced have enthusiastically become the court of last appeal." Riley acknowledged many women's desire to retreat from the conflicts in the public arena, but she cautioned them against emphasizing "goals which are personal and immediate rather than social and distant." Such a retreat, Riley said, would mean "a loss of faith in the goodness, worth, and educability of people." As women, she told AAUW members, "there are specific responsibilities we have in these critical times."[25]

Riley was especially concerned about attacks on the loyalty of teachers. Public school teachers, who were predominantly women and a major constituency of the AAUW membership, were a prime target for groups looking for subversive social influences. "We are viewing with increasing alarm," she said, "the feeling of fear and uncertainty invading the teaching profession—and all other professions in which leaders are found."[26] Riley urged AAUW members to defend public education and schoolteachers. She vehemently attacked the charge that "teachers are committed to a progressive philosophy of education which is socialistic and Communistic in its influence on American youth." Suspicion of teachers, she countered, "is a greater threat to education," and the investigations of schools and the "attempted control of them by self-appointed groups is more dangerous than the Communist threat."[27] Noting that the Founding Fathers "recognized that the success of a democracy depended upon an enlightened citizenry," Riley reminded AAUW members that as educated women they had a responsibility to guard against unjust criticisms of education.[28]

Riley's open critique of the era's witch-hunts characterized her tenure as Association board president. Serving during the height of the McCarthy years, from 1951 to 1955, Riley pushed AAUW to stand apart from the tendency toward conformity and consensus. Indeed, throughout her professional life and AAUW career, she demonstrated a commitment to nonconformity. Raised in Mississippi, the daughter of a Baptist minister and the dean of women at the local college, Riley received a Ph.D. in English from Peabody College and joined the faculty there in 1928. She later became chair of the English department and then dean of Peabody's graduate school. Described by a local reporter as "no club woman in the usual sense," Riley was only the second southern woman to head AAUW and the first Association president with a teacher's college degree.[29] Even her election proved unusual for AAUW. Riley was not on the Nominating Committee's official slate; rather, her name was submitted from the convention floor. Her popular support among the delegates proved overwhelming, and she was elected president. Only her belief in "the effectiveness of AAUW in combatting this cultural complacency," she said, led her to agree to head the organization.[30]

During Riley's tenure as Association president, the national political climate grew increasingly conservative. The Korean conflict added to the distress many AAUW members felt over the continued attacks on liberal groups in their own country. AAUW women worried not only about the "communist menace" but also about the deterioration of public discourse and intellectual life. They felt that they and members of "like-minded groups . . . [had] been put on the defensive." Their dilemma was articulated in a statement drafted by the national Social Studies Committee: "If we attacked communism and the communists," the statement read, "we found ourselves in the camp with demagogues who by their methods of attack were undermining the freedom and democracy they professed to defend. If we took up the cudgel in defense of our liberties as a free people, we ran the risk of being called communist sympathizers, fellow travelers, and even communists."[31]

In 1953, under Riley's leadership, the board accepted the Social Studies Committee's recommendation to publish a statement entitled "The Communist Threat to Freedom and Democracy." The statement, appeared in the *AAUW Journal*, and revealed the Association's commitment to rational discourse and liberal tolerance. The issue facing the nation, AAUW contended, was how to preserve both freedom *and* national security.[32] The writers concluded, "our enemy is an ideology, a point of view, a set of values, and a way of doing things which threatens to enslave the human mind."[33] Fearing both the anti-communist hysteria of the Right and the radical politics of the Left, the writers recommended that the Association chart a course between those extremes. Responding to a May 1954 attack in the *National Republic* suggesting that the "Pink Ladies of the AAUW," along with members of the other major national women's organizations, promoted communism in their study groups, legislative agendas, and published materials, AAUW asserted that "thoughtful Americans can not be harmed by becoming informed as to what communism really is." There must be, AAUW insisted, a distinction between "liberals" (even nonconformists) and "communists."[34]

The central dilemma for AAUW and other liberal groups was how to assert—indeed prove—their loyalty to the United States and at the same time hold on to the principles of reasoned criticism and dissent. The line proved difficult to maintain. Although the Association's bold statement indicated a refusal to succumb to the era's worst excesses, the pressure of public scrutiny was difficult to ignore. AAUW leaders became increasingly cautious in the wording of their public statements and even more hesitant to forge alliances with other groups. Their feelings were supported in a December 1950 memo in which AAUW president Althea Hottel told the board it was "imperative that any statement made [by AAUW] must be carefully edited for precise interpretation."[35] The members of the Social Studies Committee, reaching the conclusion that their pamphlet "Democracy Stands For" could be misinterpreted, advised branches to exercise care in using it. The pamphlet should be "chosen with careful consideration of the problems branch chairmen would face."[36]

By the mid-1950s Association communications had become overwordy in an effort to avoid the possibility of misinterpretation. As an example, the Social Studies Committee advised staff associates to use caution when responding to branch requests for materials on "What Communism Is," which was one of the committee's suggested study topics. The committee chair suggested that "the Associate should explain first . . . that the Social Studies Committee was implementing the Board statement by emphasis on the positive theme, Democracy Stands For . . . , and was therefore suggesting study and action on civil liberties."[39]

For women's groups, perhaps the most serious consequence of the cold-war atmosphere was their withdrawal from coalition work. Historically, the successes of the women's movement, from suffrage to the demands for equity in the armed forces during World War II, had come through the cooperative efforts of various women's groups working together for common goals. While each organization represented a particular constituency or focus—AAUW spoke for equity in education, the BPW for the interests of professional women, and so on—women's groups' major successes came when they combined efforts. During the 1950s, as a result of the cold-war climate, AAUW and other liberal groups began to avoid coalitions. In 1951, for example, the Association passed a strict "use of name" provision clearly stating the circumstances under which the organization's name could be used in connection with legislative and policy positions. "As the size and prestige of our Association increases," the board noted, "pressure groups become increasingly aware of the value of our support. Branch and state divisions find themselves pressed to take stands on public questions before they have prepared themselves by study to take action."[37] Although the provision was passed "to help branches resist organized pressure,"[38] an important consequence was a growing reluctance on the part of many branches to engage in coalition work.

In the chilly cold-war climate, political debate among women, and among liberals generally, became increasingly circumscribed. The decline of feminism during the 1950s was thus, at least in part, a result of the crisis in liberal institutions.

Chapter 5

HIGHER EDUCATION AND

THE NEW DOMESTICITY

A popular culture characterized by antifeminism as well as anticommunism marked the 1950s. Women's organizations found themselves operating in an environment hostile to female public participation and suspicious of women's claims to intellectual achievement, political rights, and economic equality. While women's groups historically challenged popular conventions regarding women's roles, the political climate of the 1950s, combined with a serious constriction of opportunities for women in education and the professions to severely limit the context in which women's organizations could function. Although women's workforce participation actually expanded throughout the 1950s, openings in higher education and professional advancement narrowed. Women's organizations like AAUW faced a crisis in education and a hostile popular culture both of which restricted their ability to achieve equality and an end to gender-based discrimination.

During the 1950s college women no longer represented the small, homogeneous group that had founded AAUW. Although women as a proportion of college students declined during the decade, the actual number of women in higher education increased. By 1950 more than eight hundred thousand American women attended college, just under one-third of all college students and about 18 percent of all American women aged eighteen to twenty.[1] College women represented a broader spectrum of American families than ever before; daughters of black migrants, European immigrants, and blue-collar workers joined middle-class women in the nation's rapidly growing institutions of higher learning.[2] AAUW membership thus potentially represented a wider range of women than ever before. Recognizing the vast expansion of higher education, AAUW ceased its own accreditation process in 1949 and began accepting as members women graduates of any college on the nation's six regional accreditation agency lists.[3] Where previously, for example, Association leadership had been drawn exclusively from professional graduates of elite, mostly female institutions, in 1951 Susan Riley became the first Board president from a teachers' college. In the 1950s the typical Association member was as likely to be an educated housewife as a college dean or lawyer—a vast change from the traditional membership composed almost entirely of professional career women.

The profile of AAUW membership during the 1950s suggests that postwar domesticity was perhaps not as isolating and all-consuming as many historians have assumed. It also suggests that women's organizations were perhaps not as restricted to unmarried career women as the popular press imagined. In 1955 the Association board appointed a Survey Committee to study the organization's membership and recommend appropriate programatic and organizational changes. Headed by Hallie Farmer, a professor of history and social science at Alabama College, the committee made some surprising discoveries. The findings that most shocked both the Association leadership and the press were the facts that two-thirds of AAUW members were married, two-thirds were under forty-six years of age, and more than half were mothers. Commenting on the survey, one reporter noted, "College and cooking can mix," and marveled, "More than half of them [AAUW members] have been able to find a husband." Likewise, a *Los Angeles Times* article reported that AAUW members were "far younger and more married than had been supposed." Hallie Farmer admitted that the survey contradicted even the committee's assumptions about AAUW members, saying, "We were struck dumb."[4] Studies of other women's organizations turned up similar patterns. According to one estimate, about two-thirds of the members of the BPW membership were married, and another figure suggests that even the hard-core feminist National Women's Party (NWP) included more than 60 percent married women.[5]

The AAUW membership profile that emerged from the 1955 membership survey contradicted the long-held stereotype of feminists, whether moderate or radical, as aging spinster teachers. Forty-one percent of AAUW members reported that they were housewives and more than half indicated that they had children. More than half reported full- or part-time paid employment, mostly in the traditionally female professions of teaching, social work, and health care. AAUW members were well educated, with one-third holding at least one advanced degree. They also joined AAUW for the long run; 37 percent of the members had belonged to AAUW for more than ten years. The median income of AAUW families was $6,750 per year, indicating a solid middle-class membership base.[6]

These women represented the volunteer backbone of every American community. American women, housewives in particular, may have accepted the logic of rebuilding family life after years of Depression and war, but they did not stop thinking or lose interest in public service. AAUW members were active in their churches, in women's clubs and faculty wives' groups, and in parent-teacher associations and school committees. In addition to their work in the AAUW, many were also active in other women's policy-making organizations, including the BPW and the LWV, as well as in other political and service groups.[7] That women held overlapping memberships in several women's organizations and community groups suggests that 1950s housewives and professional women saw many opportunities for themselves in public service and political affairs. It also suggests that they had consciously decided to devote at least a portion of their time to organizations specifically geared toward women and women's interests.

Despite the growing membership base in women's organizations during the decade, AAUW leaders recognized a tension between women's domestic identities and their public roles. A pervasive preoccupation with rearing children had already roused social criticism. In 1949 Lucy Howorth observed a "hue and cry over 'momism,' 'smother love' and the like." Indeed, popular psychological studies of the effects of employment on women's personalities and family roles, including those by Farhnham and Lundbert, Lester Warren Sontags, and David Cohn, formed what Howorth called a "masculine chorus . . . occasionally joined by a female soloist."[8] AAUW board members openly discussed the problem of reconciling marriage with professional ambition and public service. Board member Hope Hibbard suggested that AAUW play a role in "helping the young married woman . . . in such a way that she would not give up everything for her home." She lamented that a married woman "these days" was "of no use in the business world or in laboratories compared with a man, because after she is married her interest changes completely . . . she gives up everything." Hibbard hoped that AAUW could help women "in organizing their lives in such a way that they can on a part-time basis, or some such thing, be able to use what they have learned."[9] Dorothy Kenyon agreed, saying, "I see my own college graduates, girls who are full of zest for life and a passion for service . . . but after five or ten years you [have to] hunt for them." Although Kenyon hesitated to attribute the slump in women's interest in public affairs entirely to marriage, she admitted that "something does happen," particularly for women under age forty.[10]

The tension between professional women and homemakers was not a new problem for AAUW, but the 1950s emphasis on family and home increased the distance between the two groups. AAUW members at all levels understood the tension married women felt. Association president Susan Riley confided to board member Melanie R. Rosborough, "As a professional person who is herself leading a double life, I can understand when you say that you have reached the point where the two types of demands on your time can no longer be reconciled."[11] Many board members doubted that professional commitments could be combined with family responsibilities. When, for example, a young staff member resigned in

1951, she told the board that the responsibilities of work "can hardly be intermingled with additional family responsibilities."[12]

Family identity and public action appeared polar opposites for women during the 1950s. Few women's organizations questioned that women's primary responsibilities were to their families, but most regretted that women appeared to focus exclusively on family at the expense of larger social responsibilities. Anna L. Rose Hawkes, AAUW president from 1955 to 1963, sadly reported that "Many parents frown upon their daughters going on to college."[13] Staff Associate Winifred Helmes worried about the choices college-age girls were making after the war. Because of the "unsettled temper of the times," she said, "girls just aren't willing to put off getting married and having a family." The trend toward younger marriages, she observed, meant that "girls are not going ahead and preparing themselves for advanced degrees." The irony, Helmes said, was that "more opportunities [were] open to them career-wise than ever before in history," but few were taking advantage of them. This trend, Helmes sadly noted, was coming at a time when "more trained women will be needed than ever before."[14] Indeed, during the 1950s women appeared to abandon any claim on education. Only 37 percent of women completed college, and married women in particular sacrificed educational ambition for marriage and family life.[15]

An apparent conflict between women's domestic and public roles took center stage in many women's organizations during the 1950s. Critiques of professional women came from all sides, including psychologists, sociologists, the popular press, and educators themselves. AAUW could not avoid the tension. Anthropologist Margaret Mead observed that the tension between housewives and professional women "comes out in every aspect of the Association's work." She saw it in the "struggle between teachers who want to meet at night and homemakers who cannot leave home in the evening" and in the distrust many members felt toward the national officers and professional staff. The tension, Mead noted, was exacerbated by member perception that the professional women were unmarried, while the "amateurs" were married. Lucy Howorth objected to this analysis. Insisting that AAUW did "not exist solely to promote careers for women outside the home," she argued that the women's movement had always been aimed at "the full and free development of women."[16]

Despite public suspicion of professional women, AAUW members attempted to create, and perpetuate, a women's culture that made their organization an appealing and safe place for women who chose to step out of the era's pervasive conformity. The 1950s version of women's culture differed in important respects from that held by professional women and female social reform activists earlier in the century. During the 1950s, women's culture denoted less a call to women's particular talents and skills than an assertion of biological imperative. Both versions hinged on the notion that men and women were essentially different. However, during the earlier period women hailed the difference as a source of strength in public life, whereas during the 1950s the difference became a major impediment to public action. Margaret Mead, a prominent voice in the debate about women's role, held that there were distinctly female forms of knowledge, language, and modes of learning. Men, she told the AAUW board, were more impersonal and "nonsubjective," while women were more personal. "The thing called feminine intuition that people have talked about and philosophers have made speeches about for so long is nothing but the capacity to know that another person is different from oneself, which women have to a much higher degree than men." Women's understanding of difference and their ability to learn through empathy, she argued, stemmed from the fact that women bear and raise children. She told the board, "You have a child that is first a part of your body and then one day it is not, and it is hungry when you are not, and it is sleepy when you are not, and if you cannot figure out that it is hungry when you are not it dies." But, Mead added, "since it is easier for a woman to learn from a woman . . . everybody does not have to have a baby to have feminine intuition." Nor, she pointed out, did all women operate in the female idiom. While such writers as Emily Dickinson and Olive Schreiner worked in the female idiom, others, such as Elizabeth Barrett Browning, worked in the male idiom, which Mead characterized as entirely self-oriented.[17]

The 1950s notion of women's culture may have enhanced women's social claims, but at the same time it severely limited women's educational agenda. Margaret Mead argued for an enlargement of that agenda. Admitting that the current "model of the intelligent human being is a man," Mead insisted that women had certain "gifts" that men lacked. Most notably, she said, "men are definitely handicapped in the field of human relations." Mead suggested a model of knowledge that placed mathematics and science at one end of a continuum, biology in the middle, and human relations at the opposite end. Arguing that "women have certain unused potentialities that men do not have," Mead wanted colleges to enable women to realize their own special potential and learn in their own idiom. Women's education, she argued, should be geared toward women's and human-relations qualities. She therefore urged the AAUW to emphasize programs in elementary education and child care.[18]

Mead's emphasis disturbed AAUW members who believed that women's culture and character fitted them as much for professional life and public service as for domestic life. Kathryn McHale, for example, vehemently disagreed with the focus Mead suggested for the Association's educational programs. Before retiring from her post as general director, McHale advised that the Association focus instead on leadership training and financial management. "We have," she said, "no style for the woman executive. We have no style for the great women scientists." AAUW, she argued, should be "setting responsible leadership roles for women that they have never held before."[19]

The debate over women's role in society played out amid a growing crisis in women's education. The 1950s witnessed an unprecedented decline in the percentages of women among college students and in opportunities and resources available to female students. The crisis stemmed both from changing public attitudes about women's role and from specific public policies initiated after World

War II. As one AAUW staff member noted, "A general tendency . . . in postwar educational planning is that of thinking only in terms of men students."[20] The GI Bill of Rights, which guaranteed returning veterans a college education, posed particular problems for AAUW women. As men returned from the war and began to take advantage of the GI Bill, they created an unprecedented demand for space in the nation's colleges and universities. In 1947 half of the nation's 2.3 million college students were veterans, and "thousands of qualified women were being turned away."[21] At Cornell University, where women had formed a majority of the student body during the war, only 20 percent of the students were women in 1946.[22] Providing facilities, including dormitories and classrooms, for the veterans often stretched college resources, and women's programs and facilities suffered as a result. Women's dormitories were frequently taken over to house veterans, and class space was reserved for men first. Women could register for classes only after the veterans had chosen their programs. By the late 1940s, AAUW found itself in a very awkward position. On the one hand, the Association had enthusiastically supported the war effort and, like most of the nation, greeted the returning veterans as heroes deserving of special treatment. On the other hand, the returning heroes threatened many of the gains the AAUW had struggled to achieve in women's education. To oppose veterans' education would be unpatriotic, but to embrace the GI Bill's priorities would mean sacrificing women's facilities and status in the nation's colleges and universities. The latter was something most AAUW members could not do.

The stark decline in women's educational opportunities during the 1950s alarmed AAUW members. Although the number of women college students increased after the war, the proportion of women among the nation's college students fell precipitously. Where women had constituted almost half of all college students in 1920, by 1958 they made up only slightly more than one-third of the student body. According to one account, by 1960 "almost twice as many females as males did not attend college."[23] Even more troubling to AAUW women was the decline in women's participation in graduate education. Before World War II, women had earned between 16 and 18 percent of the nation's doctorates. By 1950 that figure had dropped to 10 percent and by 1960 had climbed back to only 12 percent.[24] Women's share of master's degrees also declined, dropping from 38 percent in 1940 to 29 percent in 1959.[25] AAUW's hard-won inroads into higher education, and particularly into traditionally male disciplines, appeared to be slipping away. Fewer women were earning doctorates in the sciences, and women had practically disappeared from the nation's medical schools. In 1949 women constituted 12 percent of medical school students, but by the mid-1950s that percentage dropped to 5 percent, a figure lower than even the prewar levels.[26] At women's colleges, too, female students seemed to be in retreat. At Vassar, for example, the number of women majoring in physics and chemistry dropped by 50 percent during the decade after the war. Women also lost ground as faculty and administrators. Where women constituted almost 30 percent of all academic personnel in 1940, they represented only 22 percent in 1960.[27]

The postwar educational crisis sparked renewed debate within AAUW over what constituted an appropriate education for female students. Although the Association had long been committed to a program of liberal education for women equal to that offered men, the postwar contraction of opportunities for women plus the growing public hostility to professional women forced Association members to reevaluate their position. Many women began to question whether a liberal program focusing on arts, sciences, and the classics was what women really needed. Some began to propose an educational program geared more toward women's domestic role.[28] This stand posed a dilemma for older-generation AAUW women who had struggled for professional status and were now teaching in colleges. Including herself in that category, AAUW board member Constance Warren suggested that the older generation put considerable pressure on young girls to follow their lead. "If they do not go on to graduate school," she said, "they are not living up to what is expected of them in life."[29]

In the end, AAUW favored combining the traditional liberal arts orientation with a program geared toward domestic skills. Board member Virginia Lanphier outlined the Association's revised demands for women's education. She emphasized that women's education should enable them not only to "acquire gainful employment" but also to "achieve a successful home and family life."[30] Anna L. Rose Hawkes stressed the nation's need for "homes where the mother in the family is well-educated." It is, she said, "up to the colleges and AAUW to see that this is accomplished."[31]

AAUW leaders insisted that even those women anticipating marriage and a family needed a liberal education equivalent to that received by men. When Mills College president Lynn White told delegates to AAUW's 1951 convention that a "feminine liberal education" meant the study of "the theory and preparation of a Basque paella or a well-marinated shish-kabob," his speech was greeted with dismay. Lucy Howorth, in a scathing critique, said, "He, like others, has missed the spirit of the leaders of the women's movement. Those early leaders were stirred by an impelling sense of justice and faith in the integrity of the human spirit." She added, "Some day in every institution of higher learning there should be a course in human freedom and the sessions devoted to the woman's movement should be among the most inspiring."[32]

During her tenure as AAUW president from 1955 to 1963, Anna L. Rose Hawkes helped redefine the Association's approach to women's education. She urged educators to gear their programs toward women's domestic responsibilities, but she also emphasized the importance of women's influence in public life. Born in Mansfield, Pennsylvania, Hawkes graduated from George Washington University in 1912. During World War I she served as educational director of the Washington, D.C., YWCA, and after the war she returned to school and ultimately received a Ph.D. from Columbia University's Teachers College. After completing her degree Hawkes served as dean of women and professor of education at George Washington University and then held various posts including staff assistant at the Carnegie Foundation for the Advancement of Teaching. In 1945 she became dean of students at Mills College, a small women's school in California.

California's postwar climate epitomized the 1950s suburban culture. As Dean of Students, Hawkes advised women college students that "this country needs homes where the mother in the family is well-educated."[33] When the Soviet Union launched its Sputnik satellite and unleashed a flood of concern about the state of American education, particularly in science and math, Hawkes cautioned, "Above all we must not eliminate any of the humanities."[34] While Hawkes stressed that women must be prepared for a variety of roles including "homemaker, mother, career woman, and community leader," she hesitated to promote either domestic or professional training at the expense of a classical education.[35]

Although many AAUW board members were uncomfortable with the emphasis on domestic skills, they recognized the practical value such an approach might have in attracting young women to the Association. Several years earlier, at a 1947 board meeting, Kathryn McHale, ever the pragmatist, suggested that the Association look into ways of professionalizing homemaking. While she personally had no interest in this area, McHale sensed a new arena in which to recruit members and retain those women who seemed to be losing interest in Association programs. Board member Hope Hibbard added that an emphasis on homemaking would serve the Association's mission of furthering practical education for women and encouraging educated women to become responsible community leaders.[36]

Ultimately, the crisis in education reinforced AAUW's commitment to provide material support for women students and scholars. Although individual branches differed in their orientation to community programs and public action and often disagreed about appropriate strategies for integration, they could all unite "to advance the education and status of women."[37] During an era that saw the greatest decline to date in women's education and the seeming rise of a new domesticity, AAUW managed to establish one of the nation's preeminent fellowship endowments specifically aimed at promoting educational opportunities for women. In 1957, for example, the Committee on Fellowships reported that contributions were higher than at "any year [up] to that time."[38]

If women were retreating into the home, they were also quietly gen-erating substantial sums of money specifically to enable young women to pursue intellectual and professional interests. The Asso-ciation's fellowship program and the activities of the branches in raising local scholarship funds provided members with a concrete program with which they could identify.

In 1955 AAUW embarked upon an ambitious plan to consolidate and strengthen its national fellowship programs. Following the ad-vice of Association treasurer Frances Concordia, the convention that year voted to establish a separate foundation, the AAUW Edu-cational Foundation, that would raise funds for fellowship pro-grams and provide the financing for a new headquarters building. The existing headquarters building in Washington, D.C., was a heavily used center for women's organizational activities, but by the mid-1950s the Association had outgrown its facilities and maintenance of the building required increasingly large sums of money.

Coming to the national board in 1953, Francis Concordia em-bodied the combination of family and professional talents that AAUW sought to promote. As one of seven children, Concordia might easily have followed the general trend of the 1930s and lim-ited her education. Instead she earned a bachelor's degree from the University of Michigan and a Ph.D. in business administration from Northwestern University. After receiving her Ph.D. in 1936, she took a position in an investment counseling firm. Six years later she became a marketing and economic research analyst for General Electric in Schenectady, New York. There, recruited by her boss's wife and attracted by the Association's wide range of community activities, Concordia joined AAUW. In 1953, like many women of her generation, Concordia left her job to devote herself to family concerns. Not content to focus entirely on domestic life, however, she began to use her professional training in volunteer activities in-cluding serving on branch and state AAUW boards.[39]

When Concordia joined the national board as treasurer in 1953, the organization's finances were, she observed, "in kind of bad shape." Association books were haphazard and, Concordia recalled, "thousands of dollars [were] sitting in checking accounts not earning a cent of interest." Looking over the finances, the new treasurer realized that the members might make more contributions if they felt a stronger connection to the Association, particularly a closer tie to the research and fellowship programs that their dues supported. Concordia also realized that the Association's vast holdings were not being managed efficiently and that significantly raising the level of contributions would require separating the educational activities, which were tax deductible, from the other programs, which were not. Programs and fund-raising could be combined, she felt, in an ambitious building plan under the rubric of an educational foundation.[40]

After the 1955 convention voted to establish the Foundation, Concordia, with the help of Lucy Howorth, found land in Washington's Foggy Bottom neighborhood, and within one year the building was under construction. Concordia had arranged for a million dollar mortgage to finance the endeavor but AAUW women surprised her and the board with their capacity to raise funds. No one anticipated the tremendous outpouring of support for the new building. "Our money kept coming in fast enough and I managed to keep the contractors bills down enough," Concordia recalled, "so we never used a penny" of the bank mortgage. In July 1960 AAUW, unencumbered by debt, moved into its new office building at 24th and G Streets, at Virginia Avenue, N.W.[41]

The new headquarters building was just one part of Concordia's development strategy. She and the board envisioned that the Educational Foundation would launch an endowment fund that could support fellowships and educational programs for women. In 1958 the Foundation received tax exempt status, and with five thousand dollars from the administrative reserve and a gift of five thousand dollars from Concordia's husband, launched its endowment.[42]

Through their work in establishing the AAUW's endowment and creating the Educational Foundation, Association members demonstrated their capacity for organizational administration and financial achievement. More important, AAUW fellowship work during the 1950s represented a remarkable statement of confidence in women's intellectual capacities at the very moment when popular wisdom questioned such abilities. Women in branches throughout the nation raised thousands of dollars to encourage young women to go to college and enable them to pursue professional lives. In 1957, just as the proportion of women college students plummeted to a record low, contributions to AAUW fellowships reached a high of $263,297.[43] Where AAUW had given only 9 fellowships in 1940, the Educational Foundation awarded 74 in 1960 and 107 in 1963.[44] In 1960 the Foundation's total expenditure on fellowship stipends exceeded two hundred thousand dollars, and within five years it had topped the three hundred thousand dollar mark.[45] During the 1950s, women who might never have labeled themselves or their organization as feminist nevertheless worked consistently in the name of equity and respect for women's intellectual potential.

AAUW and the Educational Foundation supported not only fellowships and scholarships for women students but also the ongoing programs of this active, national women's organization. AAUW board, staff, and membership had all chosen to affiliate with an organization devoted not only to women's education but to promoting women's leadership in their communities and ending discrimination against women in public life. Although some AAUW women chose not to refer to themselves or their organization as feminist, through their work in the Association they nonetheless pursued women's interests. Most branches continued to sponsor programs on women's status throughout the 1950s, and the national Committee on the Status of Women continued to debate how best to combat the prejudices and legal restrictions women faced.[46]

Women's groups during the 1950s continued to challenge the barriers to equality in education, the professions, politics, and the law. Although they were still divided over the ERA and unable to agree on specific policy issues, women's organizations united to pressure government officials, political party leaders, and local public leaders to appoint women whenever possible.[47] AAUW, along with the other major women's organizations, focused much

energy in the postwar years on compiling rosters of women qualified for public office.[48] In 1947 the Association convention voted
for the first time to endorse qualified women candidates and actively support them for elective and appointive offices.[49] During the
next two decades the CELSW spent much of its time compiling,
checking, and expanding the Association's rosters. Local as well as
national Association leaders pressured public officials, wrote letters, and lobbied legislatures, urging the appointment and support
of qualified women. Association president Althea Hottel went right
to the top, petitioning President Truman to utilize women's talents
and declare it an official policy that women be considered for appointive posts.[50]

The strategy of increasing women's representation in public office appealed to AAUW women, fitting well with their belief in merit
and opportunity. The sheer existence of long lists of names of
women and their qualifications proved that AAUW had been successful in its efforts to encourage women to pursue professional careers. The rosters also proved that many women had qualifications
and experience equal to those of men who held public office. Finally, the rosters provided concrete evidence of women's willingness to participate in public service. AAUW members hoped, as did
members of other women's organizations, that the existence of the
rosters and the presence of even a few women in high-level appointments would demonstrate women's ability and willingness to
take leadership positions and inspire other women to pursue public careers.

Because all women would be judged by the performance of those
in public life, AAUW carefully defined the criteria for the inclusion
of names on its rosters and vigilantly monitored the qualifications
of women placed on the lists. Status of Women chair Dorothy
Kenyon insisted, "There isn't any point at all in putting a stupid
woman on in the place of a stupid man."[51] The AAUW roster, she
stressed, was not simply a placement service for women; rather,
it reflected women's achievements, and the behavior of women
in public service reflected back on all other educated women. Kenyon cautioned her committee to "always use the term 'qualified

women,' " and anthropologist Ruth Benedict, a committee member, advised AAUW to always look for the "best women."[52]

The results of the women's efforts in increase their representation in public office were ambiguous. Although a few token women held public office during the 1950s, their number remained small and their influence slight.[53] The Association consistently recommended women from the rosters for available government positions, but its success in actually placing women in those positions was less consistent. Whereas Roosevelt had appointed thirteen women to Senate-confirmed positions during his first three years in office, Truman appointed only three women from 1945 to 1948. Although Eisenhower told AAUW women when he ran for president that he would "utilize the contributions of outstanding women to the greatest extent possible," his record showed otherwise. As historian Cynthia Harrison discovered, female appointments during the Truman and Eisenhower years remained "cosmetic."[54] Association board member Sarah Hughes chastised men for not taking women's abilities seriously. The chief excuse men gave, she said, for not appointing women to office was "that the women couldn't agree on a specific woman." Of course, Hughes added, they "don't say that the men don't agree either." After visiting one official to argue for a female appointment, Hughes complained, "He wanted us to do the impossible." Still, Hughes believed some good was coming out of the "constant agitation" and recommended that AAUW keep up the effort.[54]

The nonpartisan rosters formed the centerpiece of AAUW's Status of Women Program during the 1950s. AAUW membership was divided between Republicans and Democrats and women often questioned the propriety of endorsing specific candidates. Staff associate Marjorie Temple advised members in 1951, "The chief emphasis [is] on whether a woman is *qualified,* rather than the political party with which she may be affiliated."[56] The Status of Women Committee advised branches that "although a woman candidate may be personally distasteful" to them individually (i.e., may be of another party), "it is to better advantage for women in general to support the well-qualified feminine candidate." The Sta-

tus of Women Committee regularly wrote to officials of both parties urging them to consider qualified women. AAUW also wrote to
male candidates for public office, challenging them to support
women's appointments, warning that "women potential voters
outnumber the men, and they will want assurance that the utiliza-
tion of woman-power such as has been the record . . . will not be
stabilized as the status quo."[57]

AAUW women fully anticipated that the rosters would stand as
proof that qualified women were ready and willing to enter public
service. They also believed that with proof such as the rosters and
the women's extensive vitae, men in public office would see the wisdom and justice in appointing women when possible. They were
therefore continually disappointed when political leaders, college
educators, and public officials ignored their recommendations. In
1953, for example, members of the International Relations Committee were shocked and dismayed when the State Department
failed to appoint their recommendation, Mildred McAfee Horton,
to the U.S. delegation to the Social Council of the United Nations.
Committee members sent Horton personal messages of "sympathy
and concern," and the committee asked the board to "express to
the Executive Branch of the United States government its grave
concern at the continued development of a situation which discourages the nomination, appointment, and retention in office of
persons of proved integrity and competence."[58]

Although most historians point to the decline in public interest
in the ERA as the key sign of the decline in feminism during the
1950s, in fact, debate on the amendment continued through the
early years of the decade. By the end of the war more women's
groups than ever before endorsed the ERA. Both the Republican and
the Democratic parties included a version of it in their platforms.[59]
While traditional women's groups including the LWV and the
YWCA, and labor groups, continued to oppose the amendment, by
the early 1950s some AAUW leaders saw few reasons to continue
fighting against it. Convincing the general membership to reverse
such a long-held stand, however, was more difficult. Rosamonde
Boyd, a Spartanburg, South Carolina, sociologist, who took over

as Status of Women chair in 1952 faced this difficulty head-on. She told Status of Women staff associate Winifred Helmes to "by all means start a re-evaluation of the Equal Rights Amendment."[60] She spoke out publicly in favor of the ERA, although she was careful to not do so officially as Status of Women chair "until," as she said, "the Convention mandate authorizes it [the amendment]." She was so sure that the 1953 convention would approve support for the ERA that she told Helmes, "Next year will be the thirtieth year since ERA was introduced in Congress. If our Convention will authorize it we should push it through in the summer or fall of 1953."[61] Boyd proposed a typical AAUW "pros versus cons" study, which, she said should emphasize "polls, changing times, and the necessity for *serious* reconsideration [of the ERA] and a '53 mandate from the Convention."[62] Knowing how tied the Association was to convention decisions, Boyd mounted a campaign to persuade the 1953 delegates to endorse the ERA. Well aware that strong opposition still existed, she told Helmes, "I don't want you to stick out your neck. I'm willing to assume the responsibility since my term expires in June."[63]

Boyd's position reflected a general change in attitude toward the ERA. In 1953, under her leadership, the Status of Women Committee made a strong statement favoring "a reappraisal of the Association's traditional attitude" toward protective legislation. The committee argued that job protection could more appropriately be provided "on the basis of the nature of the particular job rather than the sex of the person performing the job." The Association's attitude toward protective legislation, the committee declared, "has prevented its assuming a position of leadership in achieving for women opportunity and treatment comparable to that afforded to men in intellectual, economic, social, and political activities."[64]

Boyd, her successor, Gertrude Farriss, and many other women in the Association were sadly disappointed when the 1953 convention did not endorse the ERA. After a heated four-hour discussion, the delegates split almost evenly over the issue, with 1,355 opposing the ERA and 1,219 voting to endorse it. In the end the delegates agreed to disagree, and the Association took no formal position on the amendment. The Association's neutrality was, however, interpreted as opposition by at least one reporter, who noted that AAUW remained "one of the few national groups its size to oppose the amendment."[65]

Although the Status of Women Committee and perhaps even some members of the board saw the Association's stand on the ERA as an important element in defining its political focus, AAUW members seemed less concerned. As historian Eugenia Kaledin observed, even women like Eleanor Roosevelt who firmly believed in equal rights did not consider the ERA "essential to the improvement of women's status."[66] Thus, although many historians have considered the ERA to be the central issue in feminist history, the fact is that during the 1950s many women saw it as a minor issue. Despite disagreements among Association members over the ERA, Boyd, Fariss, and others continued to advocate an active role for AAUW in the arena of women's politics. Fariss, for example, saw AAUW as being an advocate for women's rights as much as an organization of professional women.

As chair of the Committee on the Status of Women, Gertrude Houk Fariss pursued issues of equity for women in public life and criticized those in the Association who pushed for a more narrow definition of women's status. "I have never once mentioned finance folders, money management portfolios, or civil defense," she noted, referring to the program focus preferred by some members of her committee.[67] After receiving degrees from the University of Oregon and Cornell, Fariss became the principal of St. Helen's Hall, one of Portland, Oregon's, oldest private girls' schools. She devoted her life to women's education.[68] She became active in the AAUW in the 1930s, believing that the Association could serve the interests of college women if it pursued its broad program and did not succumb to the pressure toward a narrow focus. "There are far too few college women who have any real concept of the broad program of AAUW," she said. Fariss pushed the Status of Women Committee to provide "substantial programs" rather than tea parties for college seniors. "Having attended quite a few of these," she commented, "I cannot feel that they are likely to impress college seniors with a burning desire to seek out membership."[69]

Fariss pursued women's rights as head of the Status of Women Committee during a period in which, according to most historians the subject of women's rights seemed to be studiously avoided. Echoing the traditional argument that women have a special responsibility to "clean up" politics, Farris commented, "I can't think of a better place for a mop, broom and bottle of lysol than in the political arena—if we want to get something done and care what happens in our democracy."[70] Fariss pushed her committee to "encourage women to become active in community, civic, and political life." Only through experience in these areas, "and other positions often referred to as 'political,' " she argued, "will women become cognizant of and exercised about some of the 'facts of life' as they are in reference to women as people and as citizens."[71] She strongly advocated keeping women's status on the forefront of Association programs.

By the mid-1950s, however, many other AAUW women felt women's concerns could comfortably be subsumed under the more general categories of human rights and democratic participation. In 1956 the survey committee studying the Association's organizational structure suggested eliminating the Status of Women Committee as a separate entity. Association president Hawkes favored this proposal, noting that the status of women "is basic to everything AAUW does." Others agreed. One member of the survey committee went so far as to argue that "the word 'woman' ought not to be in the [committee's] name at all." She felt AAUW should "do away with any idea of segregating ourselves and our interests from those of men, for women's interests are universal."[72]

Although Fariss argued that the survey committee's recommendation to combine the Status of Women and Legislative committees "would decrease sharply the action phase of the Association program," her views were in the minority. In April 1957 she told Dorothy McCullough Lee, "This [year's] convention is very likely to be the swan-song for the Status of Women Committee." She added, "You know, I rather suspect that, if the convention does swallow the recommendations of the Survey Committee whole, a few years from this time the members of AAUW are going to be feeling a little the way the people of Portland do now! They had a good government in their hands and they let it slip."[73]

Fariss poignantly expressed her stubborn belief in the broad scope of women's rights in correspondence with her longtime friend and AAUW staff associate Frances Freeman Jalet over Jalet's desire to return to using her maiden, rather than married, name. In 1957, apparently after thinking about it for a long time, Jalet began signing her letters "Frances Freeman." Fariss told her, "In a way, it seems strange to be using a different name, and yet it is not unnatural since it has always been a part of your name. I know how you would feel about wanting to use your maiden name, for I have always felt the same about that matter."[74] Only a few months later, however, the pressures of the time overcame Jalet's resolve, and she told Fariss, "After all, I can't seem to be anything but Mrs. Jalet, so have reverted to that name—it was undoubtedly an error for me to have tried to make a change this confusing to everyone including myself."[75] Fariss, always the proponent of women's rights, encouraged her not to give up, saying, "I know how difficult it is to manage a change in name. . . . However, I think that, if you really would prefer a change, you should stick with it. It just takes a little time for people to become accustomed to anything different." Jalet apparently did not stick with it and reverted to her married name. Jalet's experience must have symbolized to Fariss the direction AAUW seemed to be taking. Upon leaving office she wrote, "The Status of Women committee and the ends which it is trying to accomplish will always lie close to my heart—and to me constitute the greatest challenge in the American Association of University Women. When the Association ceases to have major concern for the standing and status of women in every field of endeavor, it will have lost one of its greatest reasons for existence."[76]

The Status of Women Committee survived the 1957 convention by a narrow margin, but for the remainder of the decade a quiet battle continued over the fate of the Status of Women Committee and the orientation the Association should take toward political action.[77] Most members seemed reluctant to embrace an action-oriented program. Arguing that women's interests were, by definition, included in all Association activities, some saw no need for a special committee on women's status. Others maintained that the committee was essential to the Association; without it, AAUW would be unable to accomplish its fundamental mission. Among the latter group was Audrey K. Wilder, dean of women at Albion College in Michigan, who contended, "The statement that Status of Women has outlived its usefulness shows a shocking lack of knowledge concerning the basic objectives of AAUW from its very founding; also the problems of inequality American women face today."[78] Despite her arguments and those of others, however, by the end of the decade the weight of opinion within AAUW fell in the direction of eliminating political and cultural programs specifically oriented around women's status.

In 1959 Helen Bragdon left AAUW, to be replaced as general director by Pauline Tompkins. During Bragdon's nine years as general director, AAUW strengthened its adult education programs, particularly those geared toward older women. Especially in the latter part of her term, AAUW study groups thrived as educated suburban, housewives sought intellectual stimulation and social contacts beyond the world of family and children. AAUW membership increased at a steady pace of 3 percent per year, a trend that continued until 1966. In 1950 112,746 women belonged to the Association. Sixteen years later the membership exceeded 170,000.[79] Between 1951 and 1964 two hundred new branches were formed.[80] Whereas the AAUW employed twelve professional staff members in 1956, in 1964 the staff numbered sixty-five. As the Association approached its seventy-fifth anniversary, it looked quite different from the organization founded by Marion Talbot and her colleagues. AAUW's mission had remained constant, but the world in which it operated had changed dramatically. The organization had grown to meet the needs of college women in a new era.

Chapter 6

SOCIABILITY AND

RACIAL JUSTICE

Postwar women's organizations pursued women's rights and articulated demands for improvement in women's public status in a climate shaped not only by a crisis in women's education and antifeminism but also by a more general identity crisis among liberal reform organizations. Sparked most dramatically by demands for racial equality after the war, American liberal groups were forced to reevaluate their own behavior and prejudices even as they sought to press for an end to public discrimination. AAUW and other women's groups had long articulated a universal philosophy of equality, opportunity, and democracy, but after World War II that philosophy was put to the test. The results marked not only an opening of private associations to racial diversity, but a transformation in the very culture of women's organizations as well.

Women's optimism regarding their wartime public achievements was confronted almost immediately after the war by demands for racial equality within the ranks of their own organizations. Having fought for democracy abroad, black soldiers returned home unwilling to submit to second-class citizenship. Black communities, which had sacrificed their sons during the war, began to demand the privileges of citizenship that the United States so proudly claimed to represent. Liberal groups, including the national women's organizations, could not ignore the deeper meaning of freedom and equality posed by civil rights organizations. Their rhetoric of equality, opportunity, and an end to discrimination could no longer be reconciled with social practices based on segregation and racial inequality. During the postwar years, racial equality, perhaps more than any other issue, challenged the liberal identity and the culture of women's organizations.

The response to demands for integration revealed the both the strengths and the limits of the women's culture that characterized such organizations as AAUW. The very aspects of women's organizations that had provided their appeal and strength—the ability to provide a safe, supportive atmosphere where women could come together to discuss their goals and pursue their interests—also proved to be women's Achilles heel. The strength of women's organizations depended not only upon shared goals, but upon a common culture that was not only elite but was also almost entirely white. Women's organizations, perhaps more than other political interest groups, were as much places for social gathering as for political discussion. It was their social side that was most threatened by demands for integration, and perhaps more than any other factor, division over race destroyed the basis for a common women's culture. The 1950s retreat from feminism in part resulted from a dwindling of public interest in women's issues and a cold-war resurgence of domesticity, but it also resulted from an organizational identity crises that developed around the question of black membership.

An unprecedented crisis of personal identity and political principle threatened to split the organization and raised questions about the national association's role in setting policy. Although Association leaders often boasted that their organization was more than a social club, they could not deny that branch membership typically revolved around an exclusive network of social contacts. AAUW, like other groups, including BPW, insisted that new recruits be personally recommended by members in good standing. Application procedures often included visits to the prospective member's home, ostensibly to welcome her into the organization but also to ensure her "respectability."[1] Despite AAUW's principle of nondiscrimination, embodied in the myriad of study programs, legislative actions, and educational reforms promoted by the Association headquarters, the social reality of most branches remained racially and socially homogeneous.

Prior to the mid-1940s, AAUW, like most American liberal organizations, implicitly condoned the segregation that characterized American political and social life. In fact, none of the major women's organizations were genuinely integrated until after the war. The YWCA, one of the most liberal organizations with regard to the race question, faced an internal conflict over integration in 1946 when it passed an Interracial Charter.[2] The BPW's membership remained exclusive well into the 1950s. As late as 1954, only six of the LWV's eleven southern branches had black members.[3]

The AAUW's reluctance to encourage black membership reflected a fear of local prejudice and an acceptance of racial exclusivity in social and political life. Although qualified black women (those who had graduated from institutions on AAUW's approved list) had technically always been eligible for Association membership, few had ever exercised that privilege. A small number of black women became national members during the late 1930s, but the Association's unofficial policy of respecting the "social pattern of community" discouraged them from applying for membership to any particular branch.[4] In 1941 Kathryn McHale estimated that "quite a few" black women had become national members but said she knew of only one branch in Washington state that was integrated. That branch had only one black member, and McHale was careful to point out that she was "Phi Beta Kappa from Wellesley."[5] When the war ended in 1945, McHale could list only seven branches with integrated memberships including Gary, Indiana; Oxford, Ohio; Tacoma, Washington; and New York City.[6]

McHale quietly admitted the difficulties her membership had in integrating their meetings. A branch membership chairman in Oklahoma, for example, reported that her committee invited some women to join "not knowing the racial origins of those they heard were eligible." The women turned out to be black and, she reported, the incident "proved very embarrassing."[7] Through the late 1930s, McHale, avoiding the issue of branch integration, encouraged the few black women who sought to join AAUW to become national members. In 1939 she confided to Louisville branch president Leonore W. Thomas, "Fortunately, no one has pressed the idea of branch membership, and naturally, I do not care for the issue to arise."[8]

The conflict between AAUW's egalitarian principles and the reality of its practices was painfully clear to McHale. She took pride in the Association's membership standards and educational mission and frequently invoked those standards to set AAUW apart from other women's organizations. When it came to race, however, McHale had to acknowledge that, in the social realm, AAUW differed little from other exclusive women's clubs. While officially any woman with an approved degree from an approved institution was eligible for national membership, branch membership was "another matter." In 1939 McHale admitted, when asked about black membership, "Much as I dislike stating so, and which I never express in any other connection, I refer to the branch organization as social in character."[9] The question of race revealed the underlying assumption that the women's culture of voluntary organizations depended upon a homogeneous membership.[10]

Throughout the late 1930s and the war years, McHale tried her best to avoid the problem of black membership. Replying to a 1941 inquiry from the Illinois state division president about Association policy on this issue, McHale wrote, "Your letter . . . presents a problem on which I always dread to write for fear the information may be shared, to precipitate a problem in the Association which we have never been able actually to face."[11] The Association board tacitly encouraged McHale's efforts to avoid facing the issue of black membership. In 1939, after the convention met in a southern state for the first time, McHale admitted "the question has made us hesitate to accept invitations from southern branches for national conventions. . . . We were definitely apprehensive, but luckily no Negroes appeared."[12]

Although Association members tried to avoid public discussion of racial policy, McHale privately acknowledged the issue's divisive potential. Were someone to insist on branch membership for black women, she told Leonore Thomas, "the future of branches and state divisions would be in question."[13] Indeed, on the question of branch membership, McHale's fear of conflict far outweighed her commitment to principle. When Illinois state division president Mary Louise Barnes told McHale that the Carbondale branch was considering extending a membership invitation to some black teachers, McHale cautioned against the idea. "If some aggressive Negro eligible should insist upon branch membership, which would result in unfortunate publicity," she warned, "the Association would have to consider the discontinuance in all branches . . . and branches would rebel."[14]

McHale and the board were not alone in their reluctance to confront the issue of black membership. The *AAUW Journal* editor, Ruth Tyron, supported McHale's policy of following branch mores on this issue. She assured McHale, "There is nothing in the national by-laws that requires a branch to accept all eligible members who apply."[15] Other headquarters staff members agreed that the question of black membership was not a national problem but was instead one that should, as research associate Mary Smith noted, "properly be handled at the branch level."[16]

Division and branch members read the headquarters' silence on black membership as tacit approval of their exclusive policies. Mrs. Charles D. Crawford, the membership chair of the Flint, Michigan, branch, seemed to speak for other branches when she said, after receiving a request for application from "a colored woman of splendid credentials," "It would be democratic if the doors could be open to all, but I know in Flint it would be disastrous."[17] Bowing to popular sentiment, Crawford said, "If the majority [of branch members] feel that they are not yet ready to fight the battle of even semi-social equality for the Negro, then they aren't and we should wait until they are."[18] For AAUW, the question of black membership clearly raised issues beyond race itself. Association unity, branch autonomy, and the continued avoidance of conflict all hinged on the Association's avoiding a confrontation with principle.

During the war years external events combined with internal pressures to escalate demands for racial equality in AAUW. McHale's strategy of avoidance lost much of its appeal in the heightened climate of public indignation over Nazi racial policies and worldwide calls for tolerance and democracy. Alice L. Meadows, a ten-year Association member and former president of the Flint branch, challenged the Association's racial exclusivity and questioned the assumption that conflict over racial equality would destroy the Association. Assuring McHale that she fully understood the implications of the issue, she added, "AAUW does not lack the courage which should be part of our training as educated women."[19] She told McHale, "We are permitting the social aspects of our organization to overshadow its fundamental objectives." Other members, too, began to pressure the Association to confront its racial policies. Ventura, California, member Marion Draper observed, "We cannot afford any longer to sacrifice the potential capacities of any woman to the fetish of race prejudice."[20] Likewise, California state division president Marion B. Werner urged AAUW headquarters staff to give the question of black membership "serious consideration." She wrote, "We do not want to have any unnecessary difficulties, especially at this time, but certainly we must uphold our principles. . . . We must face this problem of the white man's treatment of the Negro in America." Obviously moved by news from the war, Werner implored that the Association change its attitude. There is no place "in the enlightened mind," she stressed, "for racial prejudice or religious intolerance."[21]

As the war in Europe against German racial policies pushed many AAUW members to question their own beliefs and practices, international women's groups, particularly the IFUW, began to pressure their American affiliates to end discrimination at home. The IFUW clearly stated that membership in its ranks would be determined solely by a woman's university degree and could not be revoked because of racial or ethnic background. This policy initially led to the expulsion of the German, Austrian, and Italian federations during the 1930s, when they refused to challenge racial

discrimination in academic institutions and, in some cases, cooperated with Nazi racial policies. The IFUW's stand posed uncomfortable problems for AAUW, which tacitly accepted racial discrimination within its own branches. In fact, AAUW actually lobbied
(unsuccessfully) in 1938 against changes in the IFUW constitution
that codified its nondiscriminatory policy and ensured a membership open to "university women of the world, irrespective of their
race, religion, or political opinions."[22] Although the situation in
Europe during the war cut off debate on the IFUW's constitutional
amendments, the organization's nondiscrimination policy remained clear. After the war the IFUW renewed its pressure on AAUW
to amend its racial practices. In preparing for the IFUW's postwar
conference, for example, McHale confided to a friend, "Entre
nous, the IFUW suggests we have three Negroes among our 190 vis-
itors."[23]

By 1945 experiences on the domestic front augmented the IFUW
pressure to oppose racial discrimination and challenged AAUW's
policies of racial exclusivity. In particular, AAUW members' wartime cooperation in local defense efforts and in postwar planning
groups threw them into contact with women of varied class and
racial backgrounds. Stressing the role university women could play
in organizing their communities for the war effort, McHale said,
"In a time of international strife, it is of critical importance that we
preserve tolerance and understanding toward the struggling peo-
ples of other nations. A humane spirit toward individuals, racial
and other minorities, and other nations is vital to the preservation
of the democratic ideal."[24] Throughout the war McHale's *General
Director's Letter*, assured Association members that university
women were "uniquely situated" to help with every facet of the
war effort, to encourage other women to participate, and to exercise community leadership. The national Social Studies Committee
recommended wartime branch programs that included integrated
panels and stressed that citizens' committees needed to be "truly
representative of all the interests which have a stake . . . and are in-
tegral parts of our democracy at war."[25]

Although women's war-time community activities directly contradicted the Association's unspoken racial policies, most members preferred to avoid conflict. Mrs. H.K. Painter, vice president of the Northwest Central Region, wrote to McHale, "I myself wish that our organization had the courage to admit Negroes and end this silly Anglo Saxon superiority idea, but I also realize that practically it would split our Association." Painter continued, "I am surprised that there has not been more pressure put on us, because we can have no logical reply to our present discrimination." Although Painter admitted that the Association position was weak and indefensible, she feared a confrontation would split the organization. Like McHale, Painter's devotion to the Association overrode any principle involved. Echoing McHale's own thoughts, she wrote, "I do not want to see our association split on the racial question, and the longer it lies dormant, the better off we are. . . . I should prefer not to see it raised because I value our southern branches and know that they could not be expected to accept Negro membership."[26]

The war, however, irrevocably altered the terms of debate within AAUW. In 1943, a North Carolina board member derided "the inability of women (who so blithely expect to own an international order) to rationally discuss the race problem." She challenged AAUW to "stand specifically for the thing that binds us together and respect minorities that are intelligent and well-dressed as well as those that are vocal, shabby, and ignorant." If the Association cannot do this, she asked, "are we qualified to even think about the postwar problems of races in Europe and Asia and Africa?"[27] San Francisco branch member Elise W. Graupner's sentiments reflected a strain of idealism popular among those who longed for interracial harmony after the bitter experiences of war. When Mrs. Howard Thurman, a black co-pastor of an interracial church, petitioned for membership in the San Francisco branch, Graupner went to hear her preach at a synagogue. "Here we sat," Graupner wrote, "Jewess and Gentile, listening to a sermon by an American Negro, surely that was democratic America at its best."[28]

By the end of the war, women in many branches felt increasingly embarrassed by the Association's tacit acceptance of discrimination. Ohio fellowship Chairman Mrs. Eugene M. Rial was shocked at McHale's stock reply to her request for information concerning the status of black women in AAUW. Rial told McHale she was increasingly asked "to answer intelligently criticisms from other groups that have stated that we were undemocratic and were discriminating."[29] Her voice added to the growing rumblings of discontent that had begun to surface suggesting that the organization could no longer continue its old policy of avoidance. Virginia Lanphier, South Pacific regional vice-president, told the board that branches in her region were increasingly asking for the national Association's policy on the race issue. "When I explain what the national stand is," she admitted, "they, of course, are not satisfied."[30] Graupner went much farther, suggesting that members in her branch who opposed integration should resign from the Association.[31]

Late in 1945 the Association board reluctantly admitted that a crisis was brewing. That fall the Committee on the National Clubhouse came to the Association Board for guidance on the "question of colored guests in the dining room." According to AAUW custom, any Association member was entitled to use the National Clubhouse and was welcome to bring guests. Over the years a few black women, mostly national members or international guests, had attended meetings and even eaten in the club dining room. After the war, a faction within the Washington branch began a campaign to integrate the Association and the clubhouse. They invited well known feminist and civil rights advocate Mary Church Terrell to join the branch and promoted interracial meetings in the clubhouse. Other branch members balked and vociferously objected not only to black membership but to the presence of black women in the Clubhouse dining rooms. The Washington branch traditionally felt a proprietary interest in the clubhouse and, indeed, contributed more than half the funds for the building's operating expenses. If the board accepted the recommendation of some of the branch members to restrict clubhouse guests to white women, it would be explicitly and publicly condoning racial discrimination. The restriction would not only affect guests of individual members but would limit the use of the clubhouse as a meeting place for local interracial committees such as civil defense and postwar planning groups. To accept the Washington branch's restrictions, the Association board would explicitly and publicly condone racial discrimination.

The clubhouse issue, indeed the whole question of integration, ultimately forced the AAUW board to assert national principle over branch prerogative. After the war, the national leadership in such liberal reform organizations as AAUW began to assert a newfound authority over their local constituencies precisely over issues such as racial discrimination. Questions of principle and national pride could no longer rest simply with local mores. Anticipating the federal government's stand on race relations in an age of national moral rearmament against communism, the national leadership of domestic organizations began to assert moral authority and institutional power over their affiliates, chapters, and branches.

AAUW board members only reluctantly accepted the fact that they would need to take positive action on the issue of discrimination. In December 1945 the board remained split over whether it should, as Sarah Hughes suggested, vote to leave the "conduct of the dining room as a matter for the Washington branch to decide, with the exception that national membership shall have full privileges." Board president Helen White countered that such a vote would essentially signal approval of discrimination. "If we have board action approving this," she noted, "somebody may say that we have board action approving other aspects of closed membership . . . I would hate to have anybody say that the national board approved this exclusion. That is different from saying that the board did not interfere in this. Constitutionally, that is different . . . We are in a very difficult situation here."[32] Sharing White's preference for an "evolutionary" approach, second vice president Marion E. Park also supported noninterference by the board. She predicted that, in time, branch regulations promoting discrimination would "also wear away, and there shall be general acceptance of the individual in the branch as she is accepted or makes herself accepted or acceptable in the general Association."[33] Kathryn

McHale, however, finally acknowledged that the board would have to take some positive steps. "It is time," she said, "to . . . clarify our whole relation to that problem. The requirements for our membership are an approved degree from an approved institution."[34] McHale particularly feared adverse publicity the Association might face if the board appeared in any way to condone a color bar in its branches.

The board's hesitation stemmed largely from its reluctance to challenge the practices of southern branches and risk a split in the Association. Helen White admitted to the board that she preferred putting energy toward "having northern branches go on taking in members rather than to telling southern branches what to do."[35] Virginia Lanphier cautioned branches to proceed very cautiously on the question of black membership, recommending that they act only after "a vote of the entire branch or the entire membership, and more than just a majority vote . . . so that you are not going to split your group."[36] No one on the board wanted to take any action that might be construed as a criticism of southern branches or as putting pressure on branch policy. In 1945 the board members could not yet imagine that a national board might direct, rather than simply carry out, organizational policy. Virginia Lanphier said, "We have set up our own [national] standards on a different basis and recognize no color difference, so can we, as an organization or a board, go any further than that?"[37]

Two events, however, prevented the board from entirely avoiding action: the national clubhouse controversy and the Washington branch's rejection of Mary Church Terrell's application for membership. Because the clubhouse controversy surfaced in the Washington branch, the location of the national headquarters, and concerned the national clubhouse, the Association could not easily separate itself from branch policy. Helen White admitted, "It is our Capitol City branch, and it has a significance quite beyond that of the individual branch. For them . . . to hesitate is embarrassing to all of us. This is what makes it so awkward."[38] The controversy over admittance of blacks to the clubhouse also tarnished the Association's international image. The IFUW already had been pressuring McHale to include blacks among the AAUW delegations to international conferences. IFUW members felt that "the American record in this area was a stumbling block for people who were talking of defending democracy against other ways of life."[39] IFUW pressure affected Helen White; in 1947 she expressed the importance of persuading the Washington branch members to "be aware of the possible international significance of their position."[40]

The national clubhouse controversy raised a difficult dilemma for many AAUW members: Should they demand action or use caution? One of the most salient aspects of AAUW's public identity was that they were not militant reformers but instead represented mainstream liberal public opinion. As minorities in academic communities, AAUW women had themselves experienced exclusion and discrimination. But as one member, reminded the board, AAUW women had made great strides in breaking down social and professional barriers to women by their use of nonconfrontational, subtle tactics. As one board member noted, "I know of universities in this country where I have been as a member of the national committee, and told that women couldn't be entertained in a faculty club, but there was a corner where they could go, and the men condescended to eat with the committee."[41] Helen White also supported a nonconfrontational approach. "I always keep moving slowly," she said, "but always like to be moving in the right direction." Board member Susan Riley, often described as a "southern lady," feared that precipitous board action would result in confusion in the branches and "a consequent crippling of the national program which has always worked indiscriminately for the improvement of educational opportunities for all women and for our system of public education which serves the children of all people." She observed that "the adoption of a new idea is determined as much by emotional receptivity as it is by intellectual truth."[42]

While the AAUW board and some members counseled caution, many other members began to demand positive action. Ultimately, however, it was a constitutional crisis that provoked board action. During the fall of 1946, a substantial number of Washington

Photo 1. New York City Branch of AAUW presents Woman of the Year Award to Marian Anderson, 1958. (From left) Dr. Margaret M. Bryant, NYC Branch president; Marian Anderson; and Miss Malverna Hoffman.

Photo 2. Delegates to AAUW Convention, June 1959. (From left) Mrs. W. Louis Moore, delegate from San Diego; Eleanor Roosevelt; and Mrs. Ray Townsend, from Long Beach, California, vice president of the South Pacific Region.

Photo 3. Margaret Mead at AAUW Convention (nd).

Photo 4. Coretta Scott King Award, 1969. (From left) Nell Painter; Dr. Anne G. Pannell, AAUW president; Coretta Scott King.

Photo 5. Kathryn McHale (AAUW general director, 1929–1950) (nd).

Photo 6. Mary Woolley (AAUW president, 1927–1933) (nd).

Photo 7. Meta Glass (AAUW president, 1933–1937) (nd).

Photo 8. Margaret S. Morriss (AAUW president, 1937–1941) and Helen C. White (AAUW president 1941–1947) (nd).

Photo 9. Althea K. Hottel (AAUW president, 1947–1951) and Susan B. Riley (AAUW president, 1951–1959), April 1951.

Photo 10. Helen Bragdon (AAUW general director, 1950–1959) (nd).

Photo 11. Anna L. Rose Hawkes (AAUW president, 1955–1963), 1959 AAUW Convention, Kansas City.

Photo 12. Esther Brunauer, AAUW staff associate (nd).

Photo 13. Kathryn McHale (wearing hat in center back) with WAC.

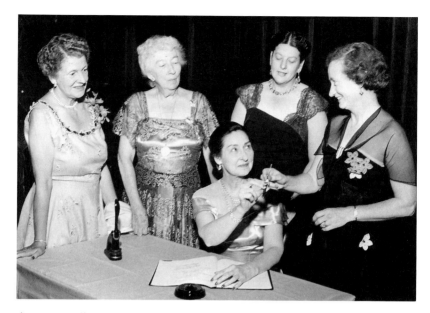

Photo 14. Million Dollar Endowment Trust Signing June 1953. (From left) Dorothy B. Atkinson Rood, Meta Glass, Katharine E. White, Frances Concordia, Susan B. Riley.

Photo 15. "Tellers count votes on ERA," 1953 Minneapolis Convention.

Photo 16. (From left) Mrs. Howard Carter, Mrs. Walter Sapp, Mrs. Courtney Smith (Elsie) AAUW Tuskeegee Branch, 1970.

Photo 17. AAUW Committee on Women, 1975. (From left) Mary Tyler, Elsie Smith, Larnice S. Eklund, Kitty M. Mason, Nancy Dean.

Photo 18. AAUW Eye Street Headquarters, 1921–1960.

Photo 19. AAUW Clubhouse Dining Room, 1952.

Photo 20. AAUW State banners.

Branch members challenged the board's deference to local custom. One of the branch's "oldest and most respected" members, Mrs. Clarence F. Swift, proposed Mary Church Terrell for branch membership. Terrell, an Oberlin graduate and president of the National Association of Colored Women, had not been an active national member of AAUW, but during World War II she began to reacquaint herself with the organization. After the war she was a regular guest at the national clubhouse. Her renewed interest in AAUW was part of her postwar campaign to desegregate the nation's capital. In addition to her appearances at the AAUW clubhouse, Terrell led efforts to integrate other well-known Washington establishments. When, in October 1946, Swift proposed Terrell for membership, the branch board unanimously rejected her application.[43]

The ensuing crisis was one of organizational identity and principle for AAUW and proved to be a searing experience for the women involved. The Washington branch bitterly split over the issue. In a branch referendum, 350 women voted against Terrell's membership and 250 favored her admission.[44] Left with a choice between decisive action or international embarrassment, the Association board ruled in December 1946 that eligibility for Association membership was to be based solely on educational criteria and that branches could no longer discriminate in their membership policies. As one woman in the Washington branch stated, "The problem is broader than the question of the admission of one qualified Negro woman; it extends to the whole question of the relation between the national organization and the branches, of the nature of a branch, and whether a club primarily social can be recognized as a branch."[45]

In addition to affirming educational qualifications as the sole criterion for AAUW membership, the board, for the first time, had asserted the authority of national policy over branch prerogative. Although McHale had long struggled to emphasize the importance of the national Association to branch members, before the Terrell controversy neither she nor the board had ever been forced to assert formal sovereignty from the center. In a major step the national board declared that "there can be no authorization for any discrimination on racial, religious, or political grounds" and announce that by May 6, 1948, any branch refusing to accept the policy would be dismissed from the Association. The board put the Association's members on notice that they were expected to "practice within their own groups those democratic principles which are in line with the Association's history, its expressed international policies, its membership in the IFUW, and its deep concern with all agencies seeking to rebuild a world shattered through discriminations and intolerance."[46] To demonstrate their commitment to these principles, branches were required to formally change the membership criteria and procedures in their bylaws.

The success of the Association's demand for branch conformity on the race issue depended largely upon the efforts of the new Association president, Althea Hottel. To successfully lead the Association through the integration crisis and one of its most divisive periods required a clear commitment to principle and an ability to negotiate between extremely hostile parties. Hottel came to her beliefs through a liberal education and a commitment to encouraging opportunity and achievement in younger women. Asserting that "we must be fully cognizant of the widening roles women can play," Hottel quietly led the Association through its most divisive period. A graduate of the University of Pennsylvania, where she received her B.A., M.A., and Ph.D. in sociology, Althea Hottel stayed on to become dean of women. Married to a Philadelphia businessman, she raised three children while pursuing her career and taking an active role in community organizations. Her energy was largely responsible for her success during the integration crisis as she personally visited more than three hundred branches and made speaking appearances in all nine AAUW regions.[47] Association founder Marion Talbot commented to Kathryn McHale after a visit from Hottel, "I think she will stand by the principle of the AAUW and her youth may be a considerable advantage."[48]

During her term as association president from 1947 to 1951, Hottel represented AAUW in the international as well as the domestic arena. In 1949, for example, she traveled to twelve world capitals with twenty-eight other leaders to take part in a "Round-the-World Town Meeting of the Air." After the tour returned to Washington, D.C., she was one of four speakers asked to make a "Report to the Nation." Hottel also represented AAUW at the IFUW meetings in 1947 and 1953 and served as IFUW president.[49]

Hottel represented the heart of AAUW liberal feminism. "It is imperative," she told AAUW members, "that we see ourselves as part of a world peopled by human beings with vastly different religions, forms of government, ways of earning a living, racial characteristics, languages, and hearthstones: as citizens of the world, struggling for understanding of a complex universe and for ways to work with one another peacefully." Committed to education and reasoned public discourse, she was convinced that the Association could weather the integration storm. She was also convinced that Association women represented the best in American democratic traditions. She expressed her views of those traditions eloquently: "The quality of a civilization," she wrote, "depends on its standards, its sense of values, its idea of what is first rate and what is not. The type of person men and women are, is of first importance to our society. Knowledge is important; still more so is the power to use it; but most important of all is what a person believes, what he or she considers good and bad, whether one has clear values and standards and is prepared to live by them. Paradoxical as it may sound, this matters more to the making of a new world and its preservation even than equality of opportunity."[50] Hottel's view of women's rights and racial justice, like the AAUW's opposition to the ERA, depended less on an abstract notion of equality than on an embodied sense of standards, values, and principle.

Despite Hottel's commitment and efforts, however, asserting a national prerogative over local authority proved a painful and complex process. As often happens in organizational crises, procedural issues quickly began to override questions of substance. Shortly before the May 6, 1948, deadline for accepting the Association's nondiscriminatory policy, the Washington branch faction opposing integration sued the national Association. The suit argued that nothing in the Association bylaws allowed the board to interfere in branch policies or to dismiss any branch from the Association. Much to the chagrin of the national board members and the surprise of newly elected board president, Hottel, the court ruled against the National board and upheld the Washington branch's claim to autonomy. The court ruled that, according to its national bylaws, the Association was, indeed, a federation of local social groups. The board could not insist upon a universal nondiscriminatory policy unless it transformed the organization into one national corporate body.[51]

Developing a national identity required agreement on language as well as compliance with legal structures. When the board asserted that any woman holding an approved degree was eligible for membership, they assumed that eligibility meant entitlement. Neither the dissenting branch members nor the Appellate Court judge, it appeared, agreed. "Eligibility and Admissibility," wrote one member, "are construed to be not the same."[52] For the Washington women demanding branch prerogative, eligibility meant "worthy of choice"; it did not mean entitled to membership.[53] The distinction was critical for women who wanted to maintain exclusivity as well as for branches that sought to maintain local control. When Althea Hottel asked her friend Owen J. Roberts, a retired Supreme Court justice, his opinion of the Association's case, Roberts advised her that the only way to resolve the conflict would be to amend the Association bylaws at the next convention. This would, Roberts assured Hottel, "remove all possible doubt as to the meaning of the word 'eligible.' " In a revealing afterthought, Roberts added, "The case is not one which can go . . . to the Supreme Court, because it does not involve any matter of national importance."[54] AAUW women on both sides of the issue surely disagreed. In a widely publicized vote the AAUW Seattle Convention of 1949 amended Association bylaws to provide no restriction on membership other than a college degree from an institution on the organization's approved list.

The crisis over integration in AAUW reflected the contours of a more general debate in postwar American public life. The ideals and the anxieties of the nation at large were reflected in branch responses to the board's action. New Jersey's Mary B. Joy, for example, commented, "Branch members condemned Hitler's racism. They regret the communist propaganda abroad. . . . They believe educated women should take leadership on the side of peaceful adjustment in domestic racial matters as well as in behalf of international peace. If the leaders in the community, the educated women, can practice in their own AAUW branches what they preach for nations in the UN, a great victory will have been won for brotherly love, and an example set for the rest of the women in these United States."[55] Pro-integration southern women, in particular, connected the Association's antidiscrimination stand to issues of national identity and international security. Susan Riley, who had been born in Mississippi and spent her career in Nashville, noted that the board, in creating a nondiscriminatory membership policy, "was thinking not only of the problem of Negro membership but of anti-Jewish feeling in certain areas, and of prejudice against the Mexicans in the southwest and . . . Orientals in the west."[56] Ruth B. Allen from Louisiana wrote, "For more than ten years we have known that this question would eventually arise. . . . As Christians, as democratic citizens, as educated women dedicated to the principle of equity in the recognition of women, we must take the stand that all qualified women shall be admitted to membership."[57]

If the board's actions reflected a shift in the direction of liberal reform politics toward centralized, professional organizations, the opposition revealed the persistence among many Americans of a fundamental mistrust of government and an almost religious fear of communism. The unity of purpose characterizing women's organizations during the first half of the century dissolved in the face of racial liberalism and anticommunism. The AAUW members who openly opposed integration did so because of deep-seated race prejudices. They expressed their opposition, however, less in race terms than in terms of constitutional issues that sounded much like states' rights arguments. Women opposing the board's actions clearly felt the national Association had overstepped its mandate. El Paso, Texas, branch president Julia Breck, for example, questioned the "growing tendency of the national board to dictate to branches and members" and contended that AAUW had "lost its identity as a democratic organization." She suggested eliminating the office of general director altogether and appointing a new executive secretary for each incoming president.[58] Another worried member commented, "The tendency of national boards, committees, and officers in almost all women's groups is to 'take over.' " She feared that the growing national staffs and the increased power of national boards was a dangerous development threatening democratic principles. "No AAUW national committee member or officer can truthfully say she represents 100,000 members," she observed. Her solution for making the organization more democratic was to take power out of the hands of national officers and boards. However, her real fear was revealed when she said, "The general public is awakening to the dangers of sleeping while subversive groups prowl. Perhaps the restlessness in women's clubs is part of the more general increasing alertness."[59]

The perceived link between civil rights and communism during the late 1940s and early 1950s had serious repercussions for women's organizations. The atmosphere of fear and suspicion that increasingly surrounded political organizations divided women who had formerly felt a unity of purpose. The division first appeared as a mistrust of those who seemed to be militantly pushing for reforms in race relations. Helen White showed that mistrust when she observed, "A good many young Negroes feel they have a cause here. We are up against a psychology that, at least in my part of the world, we are having to notice." Susan Riley and others tried to modify that view by differentiating between the militants and those who were educated and reasonable. Riley defended blacks working for reform in the south, saying, "The ones who do come are not trying to combat issues, but come for a real purpose, and not to stir up trouble. As far as I know, they have never forced an issue. We have none of the Communistic element that would want to have a test case."[60]

The confluence of integration and anticommunism was most dramatic in the San Diego, California, branch, the Association's third largest. In 1947, through the generosity of a member's husband, the branch bought a new clubhouse. During the same period, the city hired its first black teacher whom some members proposed should join AAUW. As was the custom, a representative of the membership committee visited the applicant "not knowing that she was going to call upon a Negro." According to Virginia Lanphier, who investigated the case, "alarm and consternation followed on the part of some branch members."[61] The ensuing conflict echoed that in the Washington branch incident with a split in the membership and the eventual resignation of many members.

What set the San Diego incident apart was that the opposition clearly identified communist influence as the cause of the integration crisis. In early 1948 branch president Mrs. Earl C. Rice told Althea Hottel, "The race issue is truly a great problem here because of the rapid influx of Negroes into southern California during the war. It is also unfortunate that they have been quite aggressive here through their strong Communist Party organization."[62] The branch faction opposing integration particularly feared the "social consequences of an unelected membership." Were branches to lose the authority to establish membership criteria, the members cautioned, the organization would be "completely without protection against the dangerous subversive elements in this critical period in world history." In an informal report to the board, they asked, "Do you wish to allow the immoral, psychopathic or the criminal to join the membership?"[63] In San Diego, as in Washington, D.C., the crisis revolved around interpretations of eligibility but was expressed as concerns about social custom and organizational authority.

Episodes such as the one in San Diego troubled the Association leadership deeply. Many women saw their years of devotion to AAUW and to the advancement of women's education threatened by forces outside the organization itself. Division over integration had shattered any notion of a shared women's culture and had destroyed the comfortable sociability women had long associated with their organizations. Board member Virginia Lanphier confided to California state president Helen S. Graves that she was "really grieved" over the events in Washington and San Diego. Lamenting the conflict over integration, Lanphier said, "This is a time when the world needs every ounce of constructive activity and we must spend our time in fighting to maintain the principles for which we were founded. It is really tragic!"[64]

Staff members reported a new atmosphere of tension and mistrust at the Association's headquarters as well. Staff associate Mary Smith told Lanphier that the situation was so bad that it "discourages eating in the dining room." Although Smith observed that there was "an outward cordiality on both sides and smiling greetings which would indicate that all is well," she (and others) felt compelled on more than one occasion to assure members "that differences on the membership question has nothing to do with our personal feelings."[65]

For many women in AAUW, the combination of racial crisis and the intensifying anticommunist alarm produced almost an institutional depression. Continuing reports of resentment of "national" brewed among the branches. Social Studies associate Ina C. Brown told Althea Hottel in 1950 that the morale at the recent state presidents meeting deeply troubled her. At the previous meeting, in 1948, Brown recalled, "The women were troubled, anxious, and a little frightened, but I sensed a feeling of unity and of high resolve. They faced a difficult decision, one they were not sure they knew how to implement, but there was a sort of 'God helping me I can do no other' resolve about them." At the recent meeting, Brown observed, the climate was entirely different. "I felt no sense of unity and no unified response. . . . Some faces revealed interest but others gave me the impression of indifference, resentment, and even hostility."[66] The general attitude, she said, "seemed to be that this whole business was something rather unpleasant that had been thrust upon them and they were just hoping the issues wouldn't be raised." Brown compared the attitude to the "dysphoria" that can set in after a period of intense activity. "The Association at Seattle took a high stand which somehow didn't get immediately implemented," she wrote. "There is a letdown and a measure of resentment at having been carried away by something that is proving difficult. The children of Israel want to go back to their leeks and onions."[67]

The integration crisis had, indeed, forced a fundamental, and not entirely popular, shift in AAUW's organizational direction and political focus. For many women who had joined AAUW for social relationships as much as for intellectual stimulation, the issue of integration proved unnerving. Although they were college graduates, loosely bound by their mission to unite in "practical educational work," many had never before confronted their own racial prejudices.[68] Because inviting black women to AAUW meetings meant also including them at Association dinners, luncheons, and teas, members could no longer avoid the issue. The events of 1946 to 1949 forced these women to take positive action—change their bylaws if not actively recruit black members—but it forced them to see themselves in a new light. The Association had to respond, Hottel observed, by helping members "see what the total program stands for, develop some concept of national relationships that include each member and leave them with some inspiration to tackle their own community jobs."[69] Gillie Larew warned the Seattle delegates who were about to vote on the nondiscriminatory membership policy that their vote carried broad implications for AAUW's future direction. They were not simply opening up their membership; they were embarking on new policy directions. She told the delegates that they were voting on more than principle; they were also voting on implementation. "On the first of these issues we must vote," she said, "and make no mistake, however we vote it is with the second problem that we must live. It is the second problem we must solve."[70]

Implementing a nondiscriminatory membership policy proved much more difficult than simply passing new bylaws. Most branches accepted the new bylaws with relatively little dissent. Although the Washington branch withdrew from the Association, on July 18, 1949, a consent decree ended the branch's court case and on that same day those women favoring integration reconstituted the branch and adopted appropriate bylaws. Within a short time, fifty black women joined the branch, bringing its total membership up to four hundred.[71] Indeed, reaction within the Association generally was less dramatic than the board had anticipated. Contrary to Susan Riley's prediction "that there will be a growing concern and alarm as the full implications . . . are realized," only a few areas reported serious problems or decline in membership.[72] In Houston a large group left the Association after a black woman was granted admission, and the Richmond branch reportedly lost the offer of a new clubhouse. Several branches in Missouri also reported difficulties, including litigation over the St. Louis clubhouse and concern over the Jefferson City branch being forced to "give up some of our social activity."[73] These branches, however, were in the minority.

Changing the bylaws did not by itself integrate the Association. Only a few branches actively recruited black members, and despite the board's declaration of principle, Association branches remained relatively exclusive. The fact was that the Association remained essentially segregated. Most black women were asked to join as associate members, and the few who wished to join at the branch level often applied to black branches, such as the one formed at Tuskegee, which they found more hospitable. While the national Association had declared itself in favor of integration, most branches maintained their traditional—and exclusive—social patterns. As late as 1957, Nina Miglionico, a Birmingham, Alabama, lawyer and a member of the AAUW's Social Studies Committee, told the board that "in the South there [still] seemed little question but that there was a tacit understanding between the Negro and white members, to the effect that Negroes become members-at-large and did not make a move which might close any branch, by asking to join."[74]

Although the Association officially encouraged branches to recruit black members and expand their program focus to include issues of race relations the leadership rarely, if ever, intervened when branches declined to do so. The Association board and staff, particularly the Social Studies Committee, developed elaborate materials for branch study programs on minority problems, including housing, education, mental health and community race relations. They also held up as examples those groups that adjusted their programs to attract black women, but they did not criticize the more reluctant branches. They touted, for example, the Orville, Ohio, branch, which produced a "Survey of Minority Groups Problems" that attracted new members and set an example for integration in other community groups.[76]

For southern branches, in particular, the problems of integration manifested themselves in difficulties surrounding meals and sociability. Woman-centered organizations such as AAUW, traditionally combined sociability with social action. Business meetings always included a period of socializing, whether dinner or tea, and many women looked forward to this aspect of the organization as much as to intellectual discussion or social action. Integration therefore called not only for a change in the way business was conducted in the branches but also for a change in social relations.

Branch integration usually depended upon the hard work and efforts of a few determined local women. In some communities black women did not hesitate to take the Association up on its new membership policy. In Nashville, for example, the Association branch in which integration was most successful, "it was obvious . . . that applications for membership on the part of qualified Negroes might be expected."[77] Actually, as the Nashville branch secretary admitted, "many of the [black] faculty women on the staffs of Fisk and A. and I. were already eligible because of holding degrees from Columbia, University of Chicago, and the like, but they had tactfully refrained thus far from exercising their prerogative."[78] In other areas, white women actively sought out local black women who might be eligible for membership. Still other branches, including the Durham branch, ignored the issue as long as possible; the Durham branch did not seek black members until 1955 when southern branches were compelled to respond to local crises surrounding integration of the public schools.

Two problems confronted AAUW women who sought to integrate their meetings. The first was how to tactfully and gracefully bring together women who had never socialized as equals. The women pushing for integration were not naive about how deeply racial prejudice ran and fully anticipated "opposition from some members." Both the Nashville and the Durham boards, for example, knowing the strong feelings among their memberships, specifically avoided discussing integration in their general meetings. Instead, both boards presented integration as a fait accompli and deflected general discussion to the question of where the integrated meetings could be held.

The second problem, which was particularly troublesome in the south, was, indeed, finding a public meeting place that would allow an integrated group not only to conduct business but also to share a meal. The Durham branch, for example, had for many years regularly gathered at a segregated cafeteria at which the members ate dinner before conducting business or hearing a speaker. The Nashville branch also "had been a somewhat social one," with its business calendar revolving around a series of social events including a fall luncheon, a Christmas tea, and a spring dinner. In addition, the branch served tea at every meeting. Given the social and legal restrictions to integration in most southern communities, the women in both branches knew they had few choices when it came to accommodations for an integrated group. The Nashville women found only two suitable meeting places, and the Durham branch members could gather only at the local YWCA if they wished to continue their dinner meetings.

AAUW was not the only women's organization to face the problem of finding integrated accommodations. It loomed before all liberal groups in those years. Among women's groups the YWCA confronted the issue most directly. Although the national YWCA began to encourage interracial meetings during the 1940s, dinner meetings posed particularly difficult dilemmas. In Greensboro, North Carolina, for example, although black women served on the YWCA board, they apparently "understood that the black board members should not attend the monthly dinner meetings that preceded the board meetings." In 1950, however, the Greensboro YWCA board took action and moved to include black women at its dinner meetings.[79] By 1955 in Durham, the YWCA building was one of the few places that would serve meals to integrated groups. The local AAUW board thus approached the Y and negotiated for meeting space in its facility.[80]

After the women found a suitable meeting place, they had to finesse what promised to be an awkward social situation. Both the Nashville and Durham branches conducted polls to determine how many of their members would attend integrated meetings if they included a social component. Nashville members received a postcard asking whether they "preferred strictly business and program meetings or the inclusion of such social activities—e.g., tea, luncheons—as could be arranged." About half of the women responded that they would still like the meetings to include "some social activity," if it could be arranged. Similarly, about half of the women answering the Durham poll indicated that they would continue to attend dinner meetings at the YWCA. Neither poll showed consensus, however. Fully a quarter of those responding in Durham said they preferred their old meeting location even if it meant defying national policy, and another quarter indicated that they would agree to meet at the Y but would prefer not to include a dinner with black members.[81]

Branch leaders played a critical role in steering the integration process. In Nashville, for example, the board carefully planned every step. Board members carefully arranged to bring new black members to the meetings "so that they would not feel strange." Branch leaders wanted to be sure to prevent the black women from "arriving together or sitting together" so the white members would be forced to mix with their new colleagues. "Every effort," the Nashville board reported, "was made to make the new members feel welcome, both before and after the meeting by those who were sympathetic to the cause." Although the board hesitated to serve its usual refreshments after the meetings, it did schedule the branch's annual fall luncheon. Before that event, "Key members met at the home of the president . . . and definite plans were made for these members to invite the Negro members to sit at their tables, and also to invite white sympathizers to join them." The board was determined that there would be no trouble at the luncheon. One member warned, "If anyone anticipated trouble of any kind, she was doomed to disappointment." The planning proved successful, and after this initial luncheon, "there was no question about serving refreshments at any meeting held where there were adequate facilities." Within a year black women were serving on branch committees and in three years a black woman became a member of the Nashville branch board. Even then, however, some tension surrounded her appointment. "This step [appointing a black woman to the board]," the branch admitted, "was not taken without the full consent of the board, taken individually and in a group." The Nashville experience ultimately became a model for other AAUW branches. While "some resignations were forthcoming," Nashville members assured other women, "some new members joined because they approved the admission of Negroes."[82]

The Durham branch board was more ambivalent in its leadership role. In 1955, when the school integration crisis led to an increase in requests for membership by black women, the North Carolina state division held a special conference. Ostensibly a training session on AAUW's role in the school desegregation crisis, the conference was also designed to help branch presidents and officers prepare for integration in their own groups. Apparently no member from the Durham branch attended, because a few months later, when several black women from North Carolina College visited the branch meeting, Durham membership chair Mamie Mansfield wrote to the state for assistance. The state officer tried to placate her, saying, "If you have had a request [for black membership] in Durham you see you are not the first branch in the state to have it nor are you the first seeking help to handle it."[83] When Durham's troubles reached the national office, Helen Bragdon wrote to Mansfield to encourage her in the membership process. "We realize" she said, that "the branches always have a special problem when the first request for membership comes from a minority group."[84]

The Durham board tried to follow Nashville's lead—that is, finding a new meeting place, polling the membership, and personally inviting blacks to attend. But they were ultimately less successful. For one thing, the Durham board lost some clout when it continued to hold executive committee meetings at a segregated cafeteria for at least a year after the general branch meetings were integrated. One member recalled, "We did lose a number of members . . . the branch had a rough time for about three years."[85] In addition, she said that those who opposed integration "have not returned . . . and others do not find the YWCA entirely acceptable both because of the inconvenient location and cost of the meal." Branch membership fell from fifty-six to twenty-five.[86] Durham branch programs were circumscribed—for example, the branch sponsored no study groups for several years—and as late as 1961 a member noted, "We are not yet in a normal position."[87]

AAUW's general response to school desegregation after 1954 was shaped by the experiences of the women in branches like Nashville and Durham. On the one hand, as members of an organization that was devoted to education and longtime advocates of public education, in particular, AAUW women felt they could not sit back as local public schools came under attack. On the other hand, AAUW's experience with integration in its own ranks was often so divisive and the tensions in local communities so high that the women hesitated to become involved.

This ambivalence characterized the Association's response to the 1954 Supreme Court school desegregation decision as well as to subsequent events in local communities. Response throughout the nation was dramatic to the Supreme Court's May 1954 unanimous ruling declaring that "in the field of public education the doctrine of 'separate but equal' has no place."[88] Southern states vowed to resist the court ruling. Many state legislatures passed laws designed to minimize the effects of the court ruling. Because the decision concerned an issue central to AAUW, Association members were drawn into community debate throughout the country. The Association responded as much in terms of avoiding conflict as in confirming the principle of desegregation. Knowing how volatile the school issue would be in many communities, the Association board advised branches to avoid a direct vote on branch opinion, which would publicly reveal the women's disagreements. Instead, the board advised members to "establish contact between the groups affected (Negro and white), so that if difficulties flare up there will be responsible people on either side of the issue who can talk with one another."[89]

The Association board knew that the issue of desegregation would divide membership, but the board members also believed that AAUW members could offer rational leadership as their communities debated the Court's decision. Lucy Howorth while sure that the "vast majority of our members welcome" school desegration, admitted there would be "problems flowing from the decision." She suggested that the Association urge the branches "to study the problem locally, to aid the moderates and calm the radicals and with good will on all sides work out a solution."[90] Social Studies chair Corinne Brown likewise felt that AAUW members could use their skills as educated women and community leaders to help bring about "an orderly process of change."[91] Even Association president Susan Riley, herself a southerner, hoped that AAUW branches would act as mediators in their local communities to both explain and implement the Court's ruling. She was reluctant, however, to see the Association declare a policy position that she knew many members would reject. The board thus made no public statement on the Court's ruling, although it did repeat AAUW's support for the principle of nondiscrimination.[92]

The Association response revealed a wide gap between the position of the national board and staff and that of the branch membership on the issue of desegregation. The national Social Studies Committee insisted that the Association "place itself with those who are working to carry out the decision of the Supreme Court." Committee chair Corinne Brown urged the board to adopt a policy statement that would strongly declare its "support of the decision of the Supreme Court, take note of the social stresses that might develop in some areas in the period of implementation, emphasize the importance of orderly processes in carrying out the law, and accept responsibility for leadership in helping to work out constructive programs to this end."[93] Association president Susan Riley, however, doubted she could gain board unanimity on such a statement and refused to act without the formality of convention approval.[94] Given the Association's internal divisions over race, the board stopped at advising branches "to act in a way which would preserve the stability of society and promote an orderly process of change" and urging branch members to assert "positive leadership" and moderation in response to the Court's decision.[95] Ultimately, the Association board declined to adopt any statement of policy or principle regarding school desegregation.

Riley's hesitation stemmed from her belief that the question of desegregation could better be handled at the local than the national level. She did not believe the federal government or national organizations were the appropriate vehicles through which to influence local custom. However, as reaction to the Supreme Court decision became increasingly bitter, Riley began to feel that the federal government and national organizations such as AAUW should play stronger roles. In October 1956 she wrote to fellow board member Edith Sherrard, "If we had any sort of national leadership—and I don't mean AAUW—in the past two years we needn't have been in quite the mess we are in now." Increasingly critical of the Eisenhower administration's handling of the school crisis, Riley insisted that "the President of the U.S. had as clear an obligation to exert some leadership as he does in the national crisis of war. To my mind the implementation of the Court's ruling involves a social revolution that belongs in the train of the Civil War, our two world wars and the Depression. I cannot imagine FDR—or even HST—sitting by while a whole section of our social order threatens to fall apart and passions are fanned into flames that won't die down for a generation." The president, she said, should have reminded "white and Negro, north and south, of our Judeo-Christian, democratic heritage, and our responsibility to our own traditions, of our place in the world, of our own deeply treasured values of justice and fair play." Riley suggested that the president get "off the great white father pedestal" and exert some unpopular leadership.[96]

AAUW women were not immune to the bitterness invoked by the Brown ruling. The Social Studies Committee predicted that "while AAUW as an Association would never consider any question of noncompliance with the Supreme Court judgment . . . there may be many communities where noncompliance will be considered, and considered by AAUW members."[97] By the fall of 1957 public leaders, from governors to local officials, had, indeed, vowed noncompliance with school desegregation orders. Georgia governor Herman Talmadge, for example, proposed an amendment to the state constitution that would essentially abolish the public schools. While the AAUW's Georgia division came out against the Talmadge amendment, some members felt uncomfortable allying so openly with the pro-integration groups that opposed the governor. Rosamonde Boyde, the Southern regional vice president, observed that the AAUW Georgia state board "wished to avoid the generation of emotion" that would accompany debate over the amendment, but she urged them to cooperate with state educational authorities to construct a plan of gradual, voluntary desegregation." Careful plans were necessary, she insisted, "not so much because we are prejudiced as that we recognize the difficulties arising from disproportionate numbers in certain counties and from different cultural levels, already in existence and having already had an effect on the children thereby making harmonious grouping impossible, as yet."[98]

The North Carolina state division, influenced by sociologist Guion Johnson, a longtime advocate of interracial cooperation, issued AAUW's only strong statement in support of the Court decision and in favor of desegregating public schools. Offering a "calm, objective, and unemotional approach to the study and analysis of problems," the division urged branches to play the role of mediator in their communities, to "work quietly for a positive plan . . . discourage public agitation, . . . study carefully techniques conducive to the reduction of racial tension . . . and seek to develop situations which will avoid emotionalism and ill will."[99] The division board sent its statement to various public officials, including the governor, public school officials, and the head of the State Board of Education. The North Carolina statement proved to be much stronger than any the Association board would issue on desegregation and became a model for branches wanting to promote positive leadership in the conflict. By 1957 even the Durham branch became convinced of the need for positive leadership. When many liberals in the state supported the "Pearsall Plan," which would have effectively circumvented the Brown decision, the Durham chapter opposed it.[100]

Few AAUW members left the Association during the desegregation crisis, but the conflict did feed into its general movement from active involvement in issues toward abstract study. Despite ongoing civil rights mobilization, or perhaps because of the increased agitation and public unrest, AAUW women retreated into their comfortable, largely homogeneous branches. Although members continued to press for reforms in education and in social welfare, the organization became a minor player on the national scene. The Association's legislative committee rarely initiated action, and the organization only reluctantly entered into coalitions with other groups. The issue of race remained unsettled in AAUW as it did in many other liberal organizations.

Withdrawing into its own orbit, however, did not diminish the Association's growth during the 1950s. Although it avoided controversial political issues, the Association continued to support women's education, encourage women to pursue professional careers, support wider recognition of women's potential and achievements, and assert the need for women to be actively involved in their communities and with public policy. Even though broad political issues were not framed in a specific woman-oriented context, the Association continued to represent the interests of women in public life.

Part III

MAINSTREAM FEMINISM

AND THE NEW ACTIVISM,

1960–1979

*AAUW's agenda during the 1960s and 1970s, like the
agendas of other women's organizations, focused on
political, legal, economic, and educational equality.
Although historians generally have argued that
feminism was "reborn" during the 1960s, a close look
at the programs and goals of women's organizations
during these years suggests a remarkable consistency
with earlier years. If, however, the fundamental
agendas of women's organizations changed little during
the 1960s, their constituencies greatly expanded,
forcing a transformation in the nature of the
organizations and exerting new pressures on American
institutions to treat women as equal to men. During
the 1960s, women's organizations reoriented toward
action-based political strategies that emphasized
legislative challenges, aggressive lobbying, and
grassroots street demonstrations to achieve their goals.
As the political climate became increasingly polarized,
even moderate women in AAUW began to articulate an
agenda that included membership mobilization and
leadership training designed to make the organization*

more visible on a national level. Finally during the 1960s and 1970s women's organizations renewed their interest in coalition work, particularly in support of the ERA. Long isolated by cold-war caution and historically divided over the ERA, women's groups began to reunite for a common cause. The 1960s, then, witnessed not so much a "rebirth" of feminism as its legitimazation as part of the "mainstream liberal" political agenda.

Chapter 7

THE EXPANSION OF

EDUCATION AND THE

FEMINIST CONSTITUENCY

Demographic changes during the 1960s significantly altered the constituency for women's organizations. Historically, the major national women's groups had drawn their members from a predominantly white, middle-class population that was well educated and generally middle-aged. These were the women who built the nation's voluntary associations and who sought opportunities and recognition in public life. Although organizations such as the National Association of Colored Women and the Women's Trade Union League traditionally had represented the interests of more diverse groups, most of the national women's organizations represented a relatively homogeneous constituency. With its requirement of a college degree, AAUW historically drew upon an even smaller base.

By the 1960s, however, the women drawn to these organizations enjoyed vastly expanded educational and employment opportunities, and held different family expectations than had women of earlier generations. Despite continued barriers to professional and educational advancement, during the 1960s increasing numbers of American women attended college. Where in 1960 only 15 percent of American women aged eighteen to twenty-four were enrolled in college, by 1970 the figure was almost 25 percent and in 1980 women constituted more than 50 percent of all college students.[1] Perhaps most important, more women were graduating than ever before.[2]

Accompanying the explosion of women attending college was a steady increase in the number of women working outside the home. By the 1960s more than one- third of all American women were employed, and within another decade the figure reached 44 percent. The proportion of women in the total workforce also increased, reaching 38 percent by the end of the 1960s.[3] As one observer noted, the growth rate for women's workforce participation "did not come out of the blue, but the absolute increases had become highly visible."[4]

For AAUW, perhaps the most significant aspect of women's expanding employment was the increase in the number of female college graduates who were pursuing careers. Unlike college-educated women of the 1950s, who often did not work outside the home after graduation, female graduates of the 1960s increasingly sought employment. According to one estimate, by the mid-1960s more than half of women college graduates were in the workforce, and by the end of the decade "college-educated wives were *more* likely than high-school graduates to contribute financially to their families."[5]

The new trends in education and employment reflected not only the opening of universities and industry to women but also evolving marriage and family patterns. By the mid-1960s the brief postwar trend toward early marriage and childbearing began to reverse and the nation's birthrate began to fall. Women, particularly those pursuing professions, were marrying and having children later in life.[6] These life-cycle changes had profound implications for women's social roles and political goals—implications that organizations such as AAUW could not ignore.

For AAUW, the increasing numbers of college-educated women held the promise of increased membership. In 1963 the Association eased its membership requirements and recognized women's degrees in fields such as home economics, nursing and education. Dropping the strict liberal arts requirement allowed a wider range of college graduates to join the organization. Indeed, Association membership increased from 147,920 in 1960 to 190,327 in 1976.[7]

The women who joined AAUW during the 1960s and 1970s had little in common with the organization's founders. Where AAUW's founders were a small but influential minority of college-educated women seeking like minds and intellectual companions, members a century later were part of a large group of women graduates not at all socially peculiar. AAUW women in the 1960s and 1970s represented a much wider spectrum of the nation's educational institutions and a wider range of occupations and interests than their predecessors. Significantly, where the founders by and large pursued graduate education and Association leadership had been restricted to women with doctorates, in 1980 only 4 percent of AAUW members held Ph.D.s and even fewer held professional degrees.

Although AAUW women were no longer a small, elite class, they continued to be a relatively homogeneous group that could be said to represent "mainstream" American. Most members were economically comfortable, middle-aged housewives who devoted considerable time and energy to community service. A 1980 survey revealed that two-thirds of the Association's members were over forty-five and almost half were over fifty-five. Although popular wisdom held that women's organizations were heavily populated by career women, 50 percent of AAUW members were housewives and only 32 percent held full-time jobs outside the home. Another 18 percent held part-time jobs or worked in their homes. Those members who were employed full-time generally worked in traditional female areas such as teaching, health care, and other service occupations. Their personal incomes reflected the low pay rates in predominantly female occupations, but their household incomes indicated comfortable middle-class status. While fewer than one-fourth of AAUW members earned more than $20,000, their average household income was $36,400, indicating a generally comfortable although by no means luxurious lifestyle.[9]

As in the past, AAUW represented the solid group of middle-class women that made up the backbone of community volunteers.

More than one-third of Association members said they belonged to other community groups, most often other women's organizations including the LWV, the BPW, and the GFWC. AAUW members' commitment to volunteer work spanned partisan political alliances. In 1980, 45 percent were Republicans, 36 percent were Democrats, and 11 percent were politically independent.[10] Association president Sarah Harder commented that the members as a whole "support feminist issues including pay equity and family leave; they are not partisan but mainstream."[11]

If AAUW no longer represented a professional elite, its homogeneity still indicated an exclusivity. Economically comfortable, active in their communities, and, like their predecessors, confident in their ability to influence public opinion, AAUW women were also overwhelmingly white. In 1980, the Association could claim only 3 percent minority membership. For AAUW diversity still meant a mixture of ages, geographic backgrounds, and colleges attended rather than ethnic, cultural, or racial difference. Although Marjorie Chambers, Association president during the 1970s, could happily contrast the organization's contemporary practices with an earlier time when her New Mexico state division turned down a Jewish woman for division leadership, as late as 1971 the national office had to chastise a branch for meeting in an all-white country club.[12]

Despite, or perhaps because of, the Association's homogeneous membership, national and Foundation leaders made a conscious effort during the 1960s and 1970s to encourage diversity in the organization's programs and policies. Board and staff members supplied study guides, information, and leadership for programs on race relations, housing, discrimination, and social attitudes. Marking a change from earlier years, whenever branch policy conflicted with AAUW principle, the national office clearly stated the organization's goals. For example, in her letter to the branch that was meeting in the all-white country club, general director Alice Beeman wrote, "Association policies require that all meetings be held in places where all members of the Association would be welcome to attend."[13] By the 1970s the question of whether to hold integrated public meetings was no longer an issue, but the question of how to achieve diversity in membership still plagued AAUW women. The Association Membership Committee actively recruited minority women both as branch members and as division and national leaders, but the results were mixed.[14] While branch membership changed only very slowly, the beginnings of minority representation in Association and AAUW Educational Foundation leadership dramatically illustrated AAUW's commitment to diversity.

Ironically, AAUW's success in opening opportunities for women in education and the professions bred a major challenge for the organization. By the end of the 1960s, the number of college-educated women was larger than ever, and, by the 1970s, they had begun, at last, to achieve recognition by professional organizations and institutions that had long excluded them from membership or leadership. As women made long-sought gains in their professional status, however, they began to question the identity and purpose of organizations like AAUW.[15] As historian Anne Firor Scott observed, women's voluntary associations traditionally functioned "as prolific builders of vital community institutions," providing (unpaid) careers for many women, and teaching women to be "professionals before the traditional professions were open to them."[16] AAUW, of course, had always functioned partly as a professional organization, providing recognition for women, and partly as a social center for intellectual stimulation and public service.

Indeed, the expansion of women's education and the gradual opening of professional opportunities for women had serious consequences for AAUW. Many professional women who had in the past been excluded from participation in their own disciplinary associations, including college faculty, deans, lawyers, and doctors, began to find professional recognition and a sense of community outside AAUW. The "rapidly increased opportunities for women to participate more fully as citizens and as job holders," general director Pauline Tompkins predicted, "may well have an enervating effect on the vitality of branch study groups." She worried that the leadership traditionally exerted by women in voluntary associations would be diluted. It is important, she warned, if AAUW was to maintain its reputation and credibility "as a policy-influencing association," to reorient its programs so that they served working women.[17]

Changes in women's work patterns and social roles had profound implications for the fate of American voluntary associations, including women's organizations, during the 1960s and 1970s. In 1967 Tompkins cautioned the AAUW to recognize the implications of changes in women's lives for the political landscape generally. Women volunteers, she said, "whose work was once prized because there was no one else to perform it, may now question the value of their unpaid labor in a society in which status is equated with salary." As women joined the workforce, she noted, particularly the professions, they would have less time for volunteer work. "The increased participation of educated women in paid employment and careers," she warned, "may have long-range effects in the availability of quality leadership in the voluntary association." During the late 1960s, in fact, the Association received numerous letters from members complaining that they could not find anyone willing to take leadership roles in branch work. Durham member Josefina Cintron Tiryakian, for example, sadly informed the state division president of the "painful and difficult" decision to suspend branch activity. "Career women," Tiryakian wrote, "simply do not have the time or the need for a volunteer organization."[18]

Tompkins' concerns were shared by Association president Blanche Hinman Dow, who served from 1963 until 1967. Dow feared that AAUW had become too quiet in its programs and that its members took too little credit for their achievements. She pointed particularly to AAUW's organizational structure, which she felt could not respond quickly enough to the needs of its changing membership. Looking for "ways and means of strengthening, reinforcing the overall influence of the Association," Dow, along with Tompkins, led an effort to restructure Association programs and encourage the branches to become more engaged in community affairs.[19]

Blanche Hinman Dow was raised in the tradition of female education. Her father was a Baptist minister and a college president, and her mother headed the English Department at Liberty (Missouri) High School for twenty-six years. Dow graduated from Smith College in 1913 and went on to earn a Ph.D. in foreign languages at Columbia. After a few odd jobs, including a stint as a secretary at the U.S. Treasury Department, she accepted the position of president of Northwest Missouri State Teachers College, a job she held for thirty years. When she left the Teachers College, she assumed the presidency of Cottey College.[20]

Joining AAUW during the 1930s, Dow soon became president of her local branch. From there, she quickly moved on to become Missouri state president, then a member of the national board, and, in 1963, the president of AAUW and the Educational Foundation. She also represented AAUW on the U.S. National Commission for UNESCO. In addition, she served on the National Women's Council on Poverty and the Women's Committee of the President's Committee on Employment of the Handicapped. As one admirer wrote, "She embodies . . . the intelligent and effective participation of educated women in community life."[21] When she died in 1973, a colleague at Cottey College observed, "Isn't it odd—none of the male presidents we have had since have gotten anything like the publicity or honors that BHD did."[22]

Under Dow's leadership, AAUW undertook a major programmatic restructuring during the early 1960s. After much study and heated debate, the Association eliminated its discipline-oriented committee structure and adopted a structure centered around four "areas of interest": education, community problems, world problems, and cultural interests. A representative of each area was added to the Association board as was a representative of the Legislative Committee, bringing the board to more than thirty members. Along with the restructuring, branches were called on to take a larger role in program development. Each branch was asked to discuss "emerging issues" and participate in the formation of topics for the Association's coming season. Under the new structure, the branches, with the help of the professional staff in Washington, D.C., would define problems and outline a plan of study. Pauline

Tompkins observed that the selection of topics for discussion marked "a significant change in AAUW's historical approach to program through separate subject matter fields. This change is a recognition of the growing complexity of knowledge."[23]

Women who joined AAUW during the early 1960s remember the topics as defining elements in their AAUW experience. Association programs and study groups were organized around the topics as were state presidents' conferences, regional meetings, and the biannual national conventions. The topic structure did not, however, immediately solve the problem of branch passivity. Often, it seemed, the topic approach emphasized study at the expense of action. Mary Grefe, who became Association president in 1979, remembered chafing at the passivity engendered by the study-topic approach. "What we would do in those days," she recalled, "was to get some man who knew a lot about this topic and bring him in to lecture. And being good university women we took notes and then we went home and we knew about the topic."[24] Although the topic structure included an action- or policy-oriented component, to be played out in the branches, study often superseded action. The new structure did, however, keep AAUW women in touch with major intellectual and political trends. Studying topics as diverse as "Occident and Orient" (1963), "The Growing Gap Between the Rich and the Poor Nations" (1967), "This Beleaguered Earth" (1969), and "Dynamic Learning: Releasing Human Potential" (1974), women in AAUW branches throughout the country challenged themselves to confront potentially controversial subjects in a safe, rational environment. AAUW information packets, reading lists, and study guides became valuable resources for other groups that needed information and data on the topics.

Although many Association members greeted the new topic structure with skepticism, most remained enthusiastically devoted to the AAUW fellowship programs. No other AAUW program more clearly emphasized the members' belief that women had an important social role to play outside the domestic sphere. Even though most professional institutions had yet to recognize women's potential, most AAUW members continued to believe that

if women demonstrated their capacities convincingly enough, institutions would eventually open their doors. Further, they believed
in the standards represented by these institutions and assumed
that education would lead to equality. The strongest evidence of
this belief was the increasing financial strength of AAUW's Educational Foundation and the expansion of its fellowship programs.

Through fellowship programs, the organization promoted
women's rights and responsibilities in a world in which there were
limited opportunities and continued discrimination. For many
women, opportunities in higher education and the professions remained closed in the 1960s and 1970s. As late as 1971, for example, universities persisted in admitting fewer women than men. The
Harvard Business School did not admit women until 1962, and in
1965 women still accounted for only 5 percent of the nation's law
and medical students. Women fared no better in the academic disciplines. Harvard did not grant a Ph.D. to a woman until 1963, and
in 1970 it counted only one woman among its 411 tenured professors. Women constituted only 4.8 percent of the tenured professors at the nearby University of Connecticut. According to one
estimate, in 1970 "American women still made up only 22 percent
of the faculty in higher education, 9 percent of scientists, 7 percent
of physicians, 3 percent of lawyers, 2 percent of architects, and less
than one percent of engineers."[25]

As the major national women's organization focusing on education, AAUW continued to promise its membership professional status as well as intellectual stimulation and social connections. That
status was greatly heightened for those women who received fellowships. Between 1948 and 1967, the number of fellowships
awarded by the AAUW Educational Foundation increased from
fewer than three hundred to almost one thousand per decade, and
by 1967 contributions to the Educational Foundation exceeded
three and a half million dollars.[26] That year the Foundation funded
sixty-nine fellowships, and branch awards funded another thirty-
three. Through their fund-raising efforts AAUW members showed
enthusiastic support for the principle of higher education for

women. As one member described it, "Hundreds of branches work tirelessly each year raising the funds that make this possible, even though many of them seldom if ever see one of the Fellows whom they are assisting." Individual and branch contributions increased at an average rate of 17.3 percent during the 1950s and early 1960s, "a rate of growth," the Association pointed out, "more than five times the rate of growth in membership." Total contributions to the Foundation for 1965–1966 alone amounted to $515,092.76, which was about twice the amount contributed a decade earlier.[27] Confidence in the fellowship program was so strong that in 1971 the convention adopted a Centennial Fund Goal of ten million dollars, and by 1981 the Foundation was awarding 180 fellowships each year.[28]

As part of its efforts to increase opportunities for individual women in education and the professions, the Educational Foundation established a series of projects during the early 1960s in which it provided fellowships to "young women with intellectual or productive drive."[29] The Foundation's fellowships programs also targeted distinct groups, consciously aiming, for example, to promote education for minority women, encourage international interest among its membership, and open specific professions to wider female participation. In 1962 the Foundation made its first award to an African-American woman, Queen E. Shootes, for a study of "factors contributing to unemployment among Negro home economists," and in 1963 it instituted the African Educators Program, which regularly brought women from African countries to study at universities in the United States. The program was, the Association claimed, "one of the first programs of its kind to recognize the educational needs of women in developing [areas]." In 1962 the Foundation also began its College Faculty Program, which was designed to "encourage mature women to enter a career in higher education." Funded by a $225,000 grant from the Rockefeller Brothers' Foundation, the College Faculty Program paid tuition and stipends for women seeking to pursue M.A. and Ph.D. programs. In 1969, in the wake of the Martin Luther King, Jr., assassination, the Association established the Coretta Scott King Project to provide grants to black women "to conduct studies in Afro-American history, peace, and nonviolent change."[30]

In the early 1970s, with more women than ever before graduating from college, the Foundation began to focus on those professions that continued to limit women's participation. Breaking with its traditional support for the liberal arts and academic sciences, it began to award fellowships in medicine, law, dentistry, veterinary medicine, architecture and business administration.[31] These were all fields, the board recognized, in which women were "disproportionately represented."[32] In addition, many were areas in which women could "use their intellectual talents for the good of humanity."[33]

Exercising a quiet feminism, AAUW, through the fellowship programs, tried to shape the educational environment for women. As one member observed, "Men at present, and for some time to come, will not assume that women are to be educated to take their places in the power structure of our country, in the productive and cultural creative life of our society equally with men. This, I think, is the greatest stumbling block in planning educational programs for women. Men are always thinking primarily of women as homemakers. . . . We as women, as professional women, especially . . . are thinking of women as taking their places in our society equally with men." She added that in her opinion AAUW should be concentrating on two factors, "the content" and "the context" of education for women.[34]

In 1972, to help shape the general environment for women's education, the Foundation initiated its Research and Projects grants, which were designed specifically to encourage branch activity and to involve members in educational activities. These grants funded scores of local projects highlighting community involvement. In 1975, for example, the Charlottesville, Virginia, branch received a grant to sponsor "The Firsts of Albemarle County," a community education project designed to "bring to the community an awareness of the exciting contributions of women's and minority groups."[35]

Many women who received AAUW fellowships happily recounted

the difference the organization made in their professional lives. Martine Watson Brownley, a 1978 Fellow, testified, "The AAUW fellowship was absolutely essential in my professional and personal development." A 1971 recipient, Llewellya Hillis Colinvaux, noted, "To me it also emphasizes the importance of awards for women which are independent of universities and government." Gloria Josephine Gibbs Marullo commented, "When I first received the AAUW fellowship, I was proud of it as an academic honor. Now, I recognize its true worth as an enduring statement of my worth both as an individual and as a woman." A 1970 Fellow, Carol Hamlin Kramer, recalled, "AAUW was an important institution supporting and encouraging female students in what was in the 1970s a world heavily dominated by men."[36]

Chapter 8

LEADERS OF THE

MODERATE MAINSTREAM

Many historians have pointed to the establishment of John F. Kennedy's 1961 President's Commission on the Status of Women as the defining moment in the emergence of a new women's movement, assuming that interest in women's status had all but disappeared during the preceding decade.[1] AAUW women of the early 1960s would have been surprised by the statement, for the commission was created to address the same issues AAUW members had been confronting for many years. Chaired by Eleanor Roosevelt, a veteran advocate for women, the commission was asked to recommend ways to eliminate "prejudices and outmoded customs" and ensure the "full realization of women's basic rights." The commission's members had collectively logged many years of experience in organizations concerned with women's rights. AAUW was officially represented on the commission's Education Committee by General Director Pauline Tompkins, but other AAUW members such as historian Caroline Ware also participated.

The commission's report echoed what national women's groups had been arguing for decades—that women have the potential to bring to public affairs "great sensibility to human needs." Women should, the report suggested, be brought into fuller participation in government and community affairs. For that to happen, the report argued, opportunities for women in education and employment had to be expanded, through, for example, the provision of equal pay and support for working mothers.[2] Esther Peterson, director of the Women's Bureau and a member of the commission, said, "We did not propose to restructure society. Rather, we strove to fit new opportunities into women's lives *as they were.*"[3] Widely read and the subject of much commentary in the media, the report documented continued discrimination against women in employment, law, and politics.

Discussion of women's status was not unusual during the early 1960s. Issues such as equal pay, day care provisions for working mothers, and the reform of credit laws regularly appeared on the legislative agendas of AAUW, the LWV, the BPW, and other organizations. AAUW's 1959–1961 legislative resolutions, for example, stated, "We accept as a fundamental responsibility the effort to remove inequities of law and social prejudices which create barriers in the way of full participation of women in citizenship responsibilities or which violate, in [their] application to women citizens, that principle of democracy which recognizes the human worth and dignity of the individual." In addition, AAUW pledged itself to "continued and consistent endeavor to increase [the] productive participation of women in intellectual, social, civic, and political affairs," to "develop the leadership potential of women," and "encourage full participation of women in public office and on policy-making boards and commissions," and support women seeking elected office.[4]

Branch and state division activities reflected these resolutions. In 1961, for example, the Durham, North Carolina, branch, having only recently brought its membership back to its pre-integration numbers, sponsored programs on women's status in higher education, continued its nursery school project, and regularly sponsored dinners for local women college students. Its members took part in ongoing programs on urban planning, the relationship between television and the public, and "The Position of the United States in the Orient."[5] That same year, activities at the state division level in North Carolina included conducting discussions on the impact of federal antipoverty programs on North Carolina communities, working with the state's Council of Women's Organizations on consumer education programs, and building local support for the United Nations. At its 1962 convention, the North Carolina division proudly reiterated the national resolution to "study and support measures to promote full participation of women in intellectual, social, economic, and political life, and to eliminate and prevent discrimination on the basis of sex, marital status, or age." That year, the state division diligently updated its leadership roster file and worked for the passage of an equal pay bill (which finally passed the state legislature by one vote in 1963).[6]

Although the issues addressed by the President's Commission on the Status of Women were familiar to those in the women's movement, the coalition the commission represented was a new departure. Included in its official membership was the NWP's Marguerite Rawalt, a staunch advocate of the ERA.[7] For the first time in many years ERA opponents sat down with its supporters to address mutual goals. The President's Commission did not endorse the ERA, but it did advocate measures that would ensure employment equity, and it recommended that the federal government require all contractors to "hire, train, and promote women on an equal basis with men."[8]

Encouraged by the favorable national attention the President's Commission drew, women's groups throughout the country began to adopt its format.[9] Within a short time, commissions on the status of women appeared in almost every state. It is no surprise that AAUW women, known in their communities for civic leadership, often served as officers. Anita Miller, for example, a veteran California AAUW member, chaired that state's commission. Miller subsequently led AAUW's ERA efforts in the late 1960s and early 1970s.[10] Anne Campbell, Association president from 1971 to 1975, chaired the commission in Nebraska; Alice McKee, a future AAUW Educational Foundation president, served as the first executive director of the Iowa commission; and Quincalee Brown, a future AAUW general director, served as the executive director of the Montgomery

County (Maryland) commission.[11] When asked later to name "the most visible and/or influential women's activist groups in the community," women from the National Organization for Women (NOW) and the League of Women Voters who had participated on the commissions always mentioned AAUW.[12]

Increased public interest in women's rights and in civil rights issues generally during the 1960s challenged the traditional women's groups to reexamine their strategies for organization and action. Particularly on college campuses, from which women's groups drew a large part of their constituency, a confrontational, action-oriented approach captured the popular political imagination. Influenced by the civil rights movement, students believed that nonviolent direct action would force American institutions to open their doors to all citizens. The Civil Rights Movement also contributed a language of rights and a philosophy of nonviolent direct action that began to permeate liberal organizations, including many women's groups. A sense of commitment, action, and militancy increasingly characterized the American political climate. An AAUW member commented, "What a world some college students are making for themselves." Writing to a fellow AAUW member as the National Guard occupied her campus, she referred ironically to one of the Association's topics: "Certainly in these days," she said, "we are all involved in 'Testing Values in a Changing Society'!"[13]

By the mid-1960s AAUW leaders began to worry that the organization's credibility was being usurped by the more militant women's liberation groups that appealed to the younger generation. Some feared the Association was losing ground among its traditional constituency of university and professional women and that the old ways of doing things had grown inadequate. University women, they noted, had begun organizing caucuses within professional academic associations rather than working within the AAUW. Sociologist Alice Rossi commented, "It has always struck me as odd that AAUW was not visible . . . at such things as professional association meetings."[14] AAUW's efforts in diligently compiling roster lists appeared particularly weak in light of the era's militant rhetoric. In 1969, for example, California member Ione Paradise expressed her frustration with the Association's traditional strategy, noting that President Richard Nixon had all but ignored AAUW's roster in his recent appointments to the Advisory Council on Women. "Our Roster has been for nought," she complained, "and we are just not associated with 'status of women'!!"[15]

For AAUW, the turn toward political action was at once exhilarating and frightening. On the one hand, by the mid-1960s, Association leaders saw the need to adopt more conspicuous measures if they were to attract younger members and foster new leadership. But, on the other hand, AAUW had built its reputation as a moderate organization advocating rational discourse, study, and research. AAUW women did not oppose social change; the difficulty they, and other liberal reform organizations, were facing was in finding the most appropriate and effective means of effecting change.

The militant women's liberation movement that emerged after 1968 reinforced the skepticism of AAUW women who had long worked "within the system." Those women who adopted the term *feminist,* burned bras, and disrupted beauty pageants appeared to veteran AAUW members to be extremists, women detatched from the mainstream of American politics. AAUW's older generation, in particular, had difficulty accepting the militant style. Many continued to believe that women needed to be cautious and respectable to be effective. The San Fernando Valley, California, branch pamphlet, "A Guide for AAUW Speakers," for example, emphasized the importance of conservative dress and appearance and advised women not to smoke in public.[16] A cautious approach was also advocated by Virginia division president Adelaide Stegman, who in 1971 told Association staff member Elizabeth Hull, "We do not appreciate the new informal approach." Another member complained about a recent staff visitor who wore a pants suit to an AAUW meeting and rested her foot on the chair as she spoke.[17] AAUW women persisted in referring to Association married members as "Mrs." long after "Ms." had come into popular use. Terms like *Mrs.* and *chairman,* used by many AAUW members well into the

1970s, indicated an allegiance to a less confrontational mode of political discourse.

Conflict among women over style and language masked a deeper division over the meaning of feminism. AAUW members believed that their intellectual and leadership capacities were equal to those of men, but they also had chosen a women-centered culture and organization with which to identify. They held on to the belief that women had special sensibilities that made them different from men. During the 1960s, however, their notion of women's special sensibilities and family responsibilities came under attack.

To younger women especially, the family appeared to be an artifact of patriarchy and the key to inequality, if not the cause of women's oppression. The newly founded National Organization for Women declared in its statement of purpose, for example, "We believe that a true partnership between the sexes demands a different concept of marriage." Initially considered radical by many AAUW women, NOW called not only for concrete changes in women's economic and legal status but also for changes in "the false image of women now prevalent in the mass media and in the texts, ceremonies, laws, and practices of our major social institutions."[18] Although NOW soon came to be seen as "reformist, not revolutionary, aiming to achieve change by working within the political system," its call for an aggressive legislative agenda and its militant rhetoric set it apart from the traditional women's organizations.

AAUW women initially shied away from NOW's attack on the family and its call for direct confrontation with American institutions.[19] Although businesses, government, and universities had yet to fully acknowledge women's potential or invite women into full participation, most AAUW members continued to believe that someday they would. Further, they held fast to their belief that education and merit would lead to women's equality. Thus, they were not anxious to change their approach. AAUW women deeply believed in women's organizations amd held them to be special and uniquely important in a democratic society. When the Association began admitting men in 1987, for example, Dorothy R. Cutter, a member since 1938 wrote, "I am going out of my way to express my *strong dis*approval of the recent action of admitting men into membership into AAUW. I do not approve of the present trend in admitting men into *women's* organizations and women into *men's* organizations. I believe there should be *separate* organizations, as the names imply. Men and women are *different.*"[20]

AAUW opposed militant feminism, but it did not retreat from social action. Throughout the 1960s AAUW branches supported interracial community projects, promoted education for women, encouraged women to take public office. Branches became involved in interracial projects in their communities, acted as counselors with the Job Corps, and continued their traditional work of promoting equity in education. In 1969 California member Ione Paradise observed, the "AAUW, with its study program and legislative program, is particularly prepared to be a leader in initiating and sponsoring programs for the improvement of women on all levels."[21]

AAUW resources and expertise provided important support to the women's coalitions pressing for federal antidiscrimination legislation during the early 1960s. For example, data from the Association's study of pay discrimination in executive positions were instrumental in helping women's groups convince federal legislators to pass the Equal Pay Act in 1963. This legislation realized equity goals for which AAUW had long advocated. The Association also welcomed passage of the 1964 Civil Rights Act, because of its implications for race relations and its inclusion of a clause banning discrimination on the basis of sex.[22] When President Lyndon Johnson signed an executive order in 1965 prohibiting discrimination in federal contracts and requiring affirmative action in hiring, he was, in fact, lending official recognition to AAUW's longtime work toward achieving equity in hiring.[23] Historians have tended to emphasize NOW's role in securing early antidiscrimination legislation, but NOW did not work alone. As one of the organization's founders, Pauli Murray, admitted, "Women did not come to the women's movement without bringing an awful lot of resources: resources in organizations we hadn't even thought about." She went on to say that NOW "borrowed techniques of research" from older women's groups, one of which was AAUW.[24]

In this atmosphere of increased coalition work and political action, AAUW leaders had to acknowledge that their organizational structure inhibited quick response. Because official AAUW topics could be changed only at the national convention, the board felt its hands were tied when it came to issues not specifically covered there. However, in the spring of 1968, as the Association board met at the Washington, D.C., headquarters, board members could see in the streets below the violent reaction to the assassination of civil rights leader Martin Luther King, Jr. In an unprecedented action, the board threw out the year's topics and declared a single theme, "Action for a Unified Society." General director Francena Miller commented, "The horrendous events of that weekend only brought home more forcibly the grave responsibilities of educated women to focus their talents on the problems of society."[25] AAUW, argued Association president Anne Pannell, "should be making more impact at the Association level on the crucial issues of our time, in spite of the fact that many of them are controversial." Board member Anne Campbell agreed, warning against the "tendency to want to avoid controversy." An important task for Association members, Campbell insisted, was determining how, as educated women, they should "handle themselves in encouraging discussion in a divided society."[26]

Association president from 1967 until 1971, Anne Pannell urged AAUW members not to shy away from conflict. After graduating from Barnard in 1931, Anne Pannell found herself swept into the reformist spirit of the era. She taught American history at the Barnard Summer School for Women Workers and later studied at Oxford. In 1936 she received her Ph.D. and became an instructor at Alabama College for Women at Montevallo and then at the University of Alabama. Widowed after ten years of marriage, Pannell stayed on at the University of Alabama, where she became associate professor of history. After World War II, she moved on to Goucher College, where she served as a dean, and in 1950 she accepted the position of president of Sweet Briar College.[27]

Pannell began her AAUW career during the war years, serving on the AAUW's Alabama state division board. In 1951 she became the Association's International Relations chair. Serving on the board through the 1950s, Pannell witnessed firsthand the changing orientation of AAUW women. Slightly older than the women who were raising their children during the early 1950s, Pannell's formative experiences were with women who were outspoken feminists and self-confident public figures. College women in the 1960s, she worried, seemed to "settle for so little." Although she discouraged her Sweet Briar students from becoming "hippies," as those types were "mixed up and have unsorted ideas," she told her students, "Women can do anything they want to do."[28]

The board's 1968 declaration of "Action for a Unified Society" inspired Association programs at every level. Branch programs on race relations and minority affairs proliferated. In Florida, Miami branch members assisted in funding and operating a black college library, and Clearwater branch members teamed up with a black sorority to provide career counseling for girls and a twelve-week course on black heritage. In Pennsylvania, 322 women participated in a one-day conference entitled "Thee and Me," which explored "attitudes, values, and approaches to action" on issues such as housing, education, and employment. The goal of the conference, said the Pennsylvania state division leaders, was to promote the goals articulated by the Kerner Commission's report on racial unrest: "a true union, a single society and a single American identity."[29] In a massive, nationwide fund-raising effort, members collected more than eighty-three thousand dollars for the Coretta Scott King Fund in its first year. The extent of the effort becomes even more apparent when one considers that the average contribution was only ten dollars.

The "Action for a Unified Society" program and AAUW's involvement in community projects attracted new members and catapulted local leaders into the national spotlight. Elsie Smith, for example, a charter member of the Tuskegee branch, found herself drawn from branch activity onto the state board and finally into national leadership. Although she later described "Action for a

Unified Society" as more "intellectual" than action-oriented, she admitted that the program provided opportunities for branches to expand the scope of their involvement and solidified AAUW's commitment to racial diversity and gender equality.[30]

Elsie Smith was part of the first generation of black women to become active in AAUW. A native of Omaha, Nebraska, her parents were college graduates and her mother's family claimed the distinction of being one of the town's first black families. Her father was, she recalled, a "poet and a chef," and her mother worked in adult education and home economics. In 1939, when she graduated from Omaha Central High School, Smith was one of 6 black children in a class of 350. After graduating, she went to Spellman College but was forced to drop out to take care of her mother. After several years she returned to school and eventually received an M.S.W. degree from Atlanta University. Smith then took a job for the YWCA in St. Louis, where she became involved in desegregation efforts, including the integration of the Y's own staff.

Smith moved to Tuskegee in 1961 with her new husband. There, she took a state-funded job in social work and mental health, but she soon found herself directly confronting segregation. Shortly after starting her job she attended a meeting of clinic directors in the state capitol. When she tried to use the restroom, she was told by a secretary that "this isn't where you should be." Smith used the facility anyway, telling the secretary to "find another" if she was not comfortable. Later, when the president of the meeting happily informed her that he had found a place where she could eat her lunch, implying that she had to eat separately from the rest of the members, she told him, "If you feel comfortable with me not being able to eat [with everyone else], then it's on your conscience." Smith broke two barriers that day when she ultimately ate in the dining room, which had traditionally served only white men.

When Smith arrived in Tuskegee, she discovered that there was no local YWCA and wondered what women did there. As it turned out, the wife of Tuskegee's president belonged to the AAUW, as did former AAUW Fellow Queen E. Shootes, who had become Tuskegee's dean of home economics. In addition, the Alabama state division president (a white woman) taught part-time in Shoote's department. The state division president encouraged the Tuskegee women to organize a local AAUW branch. They took up her suggestion and formed a black branch of the organization. "We were an action branch," Smith recalled. "We took all the prizes at the [national AAUW] convention."

The Tuskegee branch spoke for a moderate approach to social change. Smith recalled that shortly after the "Action for a Unified Society" program was introduced at the Alabama state convention, the state division was called upon to put theory into practice. Like many AAUW divisions, the Alabama group traditionally attended a reception at the house of the college president when its meetings were held on campus. In the summer of 1968 six Tuskegee delegates attended such a reception at a predominantly white college. The local college president warned the other AAUW members, "Ladies, I don't think you know what you are doing." When he continued to insult the black women, some of Smith's colleagues wanted to leave. Smith insisted that the women stay, and the AAUW state division president pointedly went over to sit with them. "After it was over," Smith recalled, "women were crying." The incident marked, she said, "the first big [change] in the Alabama division." After that the division began recruiting more black women.

Smith continued her work with AAUW, serving as branch president, division vice president, a member of several national committees (including the newly renamed Committee on Women), and ultimately a member of the Educational Foundation board.[31] Under her leadership AAUW became well-known in the Tuskegee community; its branch projects included desegregating the school board, refurbishing the local library, and initiating the area's first recycling project later taken over by the Boy Scouts.

Thus, by late 1968 AAUW had begun to redefine its political identity. Although some members welcomed the Association's new visibility, AAUW leaders were well aware of the resistance of other members to the Association's change of strategy. In 1970 general director Alice Beeman told California's Status of Women chair Bea Dolan, "I am only too aware of the apathy toward the new women's movement, particularly among older women, or also among the younger ones who are presently very much involved with their own families."[32] Many longtime members hesitated to adopt programs they considered too controversial. One member from the Rocky Mountain Region complained, "It seems the entire organization is becoming more and more political and trying to compete with NOW and the League of Women Voters." Most women in her branch, she noted, were "more concerned with providing funds for a local scholarship."[33] Another member commented that the Association tended "to deal too heavily in political matters." She continued, "We do not care to be labeled as an organization who stands for certain legislative actions but are willing to be an educational organization helping to inform our members as well as the community to the pros and cons to various issues."[34] Alice Beeman disagreed. Reflecting the sentiments of many Association leaders, she said, "My own feeling is that if we do not change, we will die."[35]

AAUW members' ambivalence regarding political style and strategy revealed even deeper divisions over the era's central political issues. On one of the critical new feminist issues—abortion rights—AAUW members reached relative agreement. According to a 1970 member poll, 70 percent of AAUW women favored the legalization of abortion.[36] But feminism's old nemesis, the ERA, continued to divide the organization. A 1971 poll, for example, found that only 53.8 percent of the members favored the ERA while 44.5 continued to oppose the amendment. AAUW members were, in fact, more divided over the ERA than they were over the war in Vietnam. In the same 1971 poll, 66 percent of the members favored withdrawal from Vietnam while 30.6 percent favored a continued U.S. presence there.[37]

The AAUW proved to be one of the last women's groups to endorse the ERA.[38] by 1970 most other national women's groups had come out in favor of the amendment and the fledgling NOW adopted the ERA as its central issue. Opposition to the amendment virtually dissolved when the influential United Auto Workers Union endorsed it, and, in 1970 the House of Representatives finally approved the ERA.[39] The ERA quickly became such a powerful symbol of feminism that women joining AAUW often assumed the Association supported the amendment and were surprised to hear the organization still had taken no position on the issue. California division president Ione Paradise spoke for many others when she told Alice Beeman of her "embarrassment" at the Association's stand.[40]

AAUW's 1971 convention proved a turning point. That year the convention voted overwhelmingly to endorse the ERA, declaring it a top AAUW priority. The convention also passed a resolution "to work for the repeal of restrictive laws on abortion, making abortion legal for those who wish it after medical consultation."[41] Joan Hayes, the Hawaii division legislative chair, declared, "Women are coming to realize that the right to control their bodies is as important as the right to vote."[42] These decisions galvanized the AAUW membership and reinvigorated programs at every level. Association president Anne Campbell praised the convention action and urged AAUW members to help their communities "seek nonmilitant routes to equality in keeping with our tradition of special responsibility." AAUW, she commented, "must play a more active role in the national process of reordering priorities . . . the Association must give leadership—and a moderate voice—to efforts to secure a wide range of alternatives for women."[43] She saw AAUW as a leader in reconciling moderate, mainstream feminism with the new spirit of the women's movement.[44]

As the Association's first president who made her career in public education, Campbell saw AAUW's mission as helping women find "nonmilitant routes to equality."[45] Raised on a ranch in southern Colorado, Campbell developed the virtues of independence and self-confidence. Her personal background could not mitigate social norms, however, when, as a newlywed fresh out of college, she discovered that married women could not teach school. During World War II school systems began to hire married women, but Campbell found that although she could teach in the same system as her husband she could not teach in the same building. As a physical education teacher, Campbell combined her love of sports with her commitment to education. In addition to teaching, she played semi-professional basketball for almost three years.

When her youngest child was in fifth grade, Campbell was appointed to fill a vacancy in the office of the county superintendent of schools. The job increased her interest in education, and she returned to school to get a master's degree in that field. "I really wanted to be a rancher," she commented, "but women weren't allowed in animal science." Campbell rapidly moved up in the State Department of Education, eventually becoming Nebraska's commissioner of education, the highest post in the state held by a woman. She also moved quickly into leadership in AAUW. She had joined AAUW during World War II, attracted to the organization's social projects, cultural arts, and programs in international relations. By 1952 she had become president of the Nebraska division. She described AAUW women as "truly educated women who can communicate with anybody." She believed that for AAUW women education was not "a badge of honor"; it was a "badge of service."[46]

Campbell became an activist within the organization. She lobbied her state legislature for the Association's educational program, including the establishment of public kindergartens. She also challenged the AAUW to change from within. Lobbying among members, she promoted regional diversity on the board and encouraged the formation of networks with other associations.[47] During the 1960s Campbell chaired the state's Status of Women Commission under four Nebraska governors. In 1971 she was instrumental in the Association's approval of the ERA.

Once the 1971 convention endorsed the ERA and reproductive rights, AAUW became a vocal member of the national feminist coalition. Association members lent credibility to demands for women's equality and appealed to the stratum of Americans, both men and women, who believed in equal rights but remained suspicious of the more radical youth movements of the era. Revealing their mainstream roots, for example, AAUW women in 1975 proposed, as part of their ERA Florida strategy, that members write notes to the wives of state legislators that began, "I am sure for years your husband has depended on you for sound advice and counsel."[48]

AAUW women were, of course, not new to lobbying and legislative reform, and in the 1970s they provided crucial expertise in the formulation of landmark legislation designed to ensure equity in education. AAUW became an important voice in the coalition that successfully promoted Title IX of the Educational Amendments in 1972 and the Women's Educational Equity Act (WEEA) in 1974. Realizing AAUW's original goal of opening opportunities for women in the nation's educational institutions Title IX outlawed sex discrimination in any educational program or activity receiving federal funds, and WEEA provided funds for research and development to support equity in education.[49] AAUW saw in the passage of this legislation, and in the growing number of affirmative action decisions, acknowledgment of its fundamental mission.

However, achieving equity for women students was only part of AAUW's mission; the organization also pursued equity for women college faculty. During the 1970s, as the Association gained increasing visibility in the women's movement, university women began to turn once again to AAUW for support in their efforts to secure equity in salaries, promotions, and tenure. Women on the nations university and college campuses faced continued second-class status. A 1976 Association study, for example, found that although the number of female college students had increased over the past ten years, the status of women faculty members had not improved. Only 4 percent of university administrative positions were held by women in 1976, and a gender gap persisted in faculty salaries.[50] In 1977 general director Helen Wolfe noted that increasing numbers of faculty women were writing to her concerning discrimination in hiring and promotion and lamented that the Association no longer had any formal means of addressing these problems. "They ask for help in their battles," she said, "but thus far the Association has done little more in their behalf than write letters of protest." Wolfe and other board members began to discuss the possibility of establishing a legal defense fund to assist women faculty who filed discrimination suits. Without establishing such a fund, she said, "we can only say 'Right on, sister, but don't ask us to share your ordeal." She added, "Do we then wonder that many women faculty members do not find in AAUW what they are looking for? Who today can speak for academic women if we do not?"[51] Within a few years the Association formalized its support for faculty antidiscrimination suits by establishing the AAUW Legal Advocacy Fund.

During the 1970s AAUW, with its resources, staff, and expertise, was well positioned to become a central player in the expanding feminist coalition. In particular, it focused its energies on the ERA. The LWV, BPW, GFWC, AAUW, and other groups together engineered what one source called "a sophisticated endeavor" of divided responsibilities and well-coordinated political activities on the state and national levels.[52] In Indiana, for example, the AAUW state president used both political and family connections to gain Republican Party support for the amendment.[53] Exemplifying the coalition's joint work, the AAUW's ERA Ad Hoc Committee coordinated efforts with other organizations to mobilize women in key states including Illinois, Indiana, Missouri, and Florida. "I think we have a "new army," commented one committee member. "The response . . . has been very gratifying!"[54] AAUW also became a stalwart in the ERAmerica coalition, a clearinghouse for information and funding for state ERA campaigns.[55] In addition, the Association's staff regularly provided technical assistance to groups developing ERA materials and strategies, and in California, Anita Miller and other AAUW members spent hundreds of hours lobbying their state legislators to support ratification. Helen Wolfe, observed, "AAUW action has been the only effort by a major organization. . . . If nothing else, we should be able to take credit for refusing to let the issue die."[56] In 1977, the AAUW became the first national organization to support NOW's proposal to extend the ERA ratification deadline.[57]

AAUW's enthusiastic support for the ERA reflected an important shift that had occurred in the definition of feminism and in the strategic goals of women's organizations. AAUW's view of women's rights traditionally had been tied to a faith in individual merit and achievement, but by 1977, despite women's achievements in education and their now-permanent place in the workforce, the old discriminations had not disappeared. It seemed that merit and achievement were not enough. Women still earned fifty-nine cents for every dollar men brought home; divorce laws, credit practices, and property settlements still favored men; and in some states women were still subjected to special provisions in jury service. "The current constitutional guarantees," noted AAUW's Ad Hoc ERA Committee, "have proved to be ineffective in securing equality for the majority of our population because they do not forbid arbitrary discrimination based on sex."[58] During the long period of public opposition to the ERA, the women's movement had assumed that working-class women needed legal protections against unscrupulous employers. By the 1970s, middle-class women also found themselves vulnerable and sought constitutional protection against continuing discrimination. Although most women sought no special protection from unjust working conditions, they still, it appeared, needed protection from an unjust legal system and an economy based upon discrimination. For AAUW women, in particular, passage of the ERA would signal a positive affirmation of women's potential and the legal compulsion to level the competitive playing field. The ERA would ensure, the Ad Hoc Committee insisted, that women "be considered on an equal basis with men for admission to state supported schools," and that "all courses must be made available to both sexes."[59]

Like its support for the ERA, AAUW's position on reproductive rights in the 1960s and 1970s reflected a shift in the definition and scope of American feminism. During the 1930s, when the Association faced the controversy over birth control, even the most militant feminists focused almost exclusively on legal rights, economic opportunity, and political participation. Although a few groups, such as Margaret Sanger's Birth Control League, addressed women's reproductive lives, most women's organizations, including those defining themselves as feminist, did not emphasize individual behavior or challenge the assumption that women held a special relationship to the family. AAUW's approach to feminism concentrated on women's right to education, a career, and political recognition. By the 1970s, however, although educational and career opportunities slowly began to open and legal obstacles to equality had begun to disappear, women still found themselves to be second-class citizens. It became apparent, even to many women in AAUW's middle-class membership, that something more than the legal system needed to change. Women began to see the need to change individual attitudes and behavior as well as public opportunities. They began to speak for fundamental changes in personal relationships and family roles. Betty Friedan, trying to convince veteran feminist Marguerite Rawalt to support NOW, observed, "Some of the issues that concern them [the new feminists] as much as employment discrimination and the equal rights amendment seem to irritate you; but to them, and I must admit increasingly to me, these two kinds of issues are in effect indivisible. . . . To be blunt, the New Woman whom NOW speaks for . . . insists on an honest confrontation of the sexual implications of full equality . . . and sees these sexual issues not as irrelevant but as indispensable to true equality in employment and the body politic."[60]

In 1975 Association president Marjorie Bell Chambers articulated her understanding of feminism's goal as "an androgynous society of fully liberated persons committed to the cause: peace on earth and goodwill to all people through an integrated society that welcomes diversity."[61] Eschewing the angry militancy of women's liberation, she nonetheless pushed AAUW to become politically visible and take on a leadership role in the feminist movement.[62] Serving as Association president from 1975 to 1979, she had ambitious goals for the organization.

Raised in New England, Chambers said she became the "son my father never had." Her father, who held John Stuart Mill and Abraham Lincoln as heroes, was active in the American Legion and other civic clubs. Her mother did not go to college but insisted that Marjorie and her sister attend Mount Holyoke. There, she majored in history, minored in political science, and spent the rest of her time playing field hockey and tennis, skiing, and figure skating. On the morning of her senior graduation breakfast in December 1943, she, like all the graduates, received a folder that contained information about AAUW. She was told to keep the membership application card, "put it away with your jewelry, [for] you may want it sometime."

Chambers's career was shaped by the events of World War II. After graduating from college she briefly attended a Katherine Gibbs secretarial school, but she left when she found it "stuffy." She joined the staff of Clark Eikleberg, head of the League of Nations Association, three days before the Dumbarton Oaks proposals announcing the United Nations were put forward. "I took them [the proposals] down from Washington . . . in shorthand over the telephone," she recalled, "eight carbon copies." It was her first experience in a long career in international relations.

Chambers' thoughts returned to graduation day and her AAUW card when in 1950, as a housewife in Los Alamos, New Mexico, she saw a notice announcing the charter meeting of the Los Alamos AAUW branch. Attending the meeting, she heard an older woman discuss "the same theme" on which her father had raised her, "to whom much is given much is required." The speaker's words about the responsibility of women with higher education to "go out and do something for our community" convinced Chambers to join the Association. She also admitted another motivation, however—one shared by many other postwar housewives. "I had been in town since May," she recalled, "with two infants. I was going nuts. It offered me a chance to at least keep my brain going." Within a year Chambers had become program vice president and then president of the branch. In its first few years the branch started a preschool, established a cancer clinic for Pap tests, and began a friends-of-the-public-library organization. "We were to be catalysts in our community," she said. At the time that Chambers became active in AAUW, the organization's leadership was still dominated by women with Ph.D.'s, and in 1958, when she served on the Association's International Relations Committee, she was one of the few women without a higher degree. "Committees in those days," she recalled, "were all Ph.D. faculty." Chambers ultimately returned to school to receive a doctorate in history from the University of New Mexico. She became Association president in 1975. Like Anne Campbell, she provided leadership in a time of transition. According to Chambers, the AAUW was moving "from a collection of quiet study groups into a grassroots community organization."[63]

General director Helen Wolfe, addressing the Association's 1977 convention, acknowledged the transformation in AAUW. The Association had moved, she said, from "a woman's organization to feminism." The difference, as she saw it, was one of orientation. A woman's organization, she argued, is "largely content with the status quo, is socially oriented, concerned with civic activities and study for self-improvement." A feminist organization "is concerned with the equality of women and the full role of women in society." By her own definition, of course, AAUW had always been a feminist organization, but it had not always adopted strategies and programs directly aimed at political action toward those goals. If the Association were to assert itself in the new political arena, she assured members, "then AAUW will have no competition in attracting and mobilizing the best and the brightest women in this country who can bring their training to bear to work for the betterment of all women."[64]

Wolfe admitted that she had been receiving "sharply mixed signals" from Association members about the AAUW's new orientation. Some women complained that the Association was becoming too political; others felt it was not active enough. Wolfe recalled her recent experience at a dinner celebrating the eighty-fifth anniversary of an AAUW branch. The dinner was scheduled to be held in a club that did not allow women to use the front entrance. To reach the private dining room, Wolfe reported, "women had to use the side entrance." Some branch women, offended by the club's policy, complained to Wolfe and to the Association president, Marjorie Chambers. Wolfe and Chambers decided to "take action," and as an act of protest they entered the club through the front entrance. "What was surprising," said Wolfe, "was the reaction of the women in the branch. The ones who had complained about the injustice would not come and support us in this action. The others, as expected, used the side entrance and then acted as if the incident had not occurred, in a replay of 'the Emperor's New Clothes.' " Wolfe warned that without "a consistent self image" the Association could not "have a consistent public image."[65]

By the late 1970s, however, changes in the American political climate and the strong commitment of the Association's leaders pushed AAUW members to affirm the organization's new public image. Adopting the era's preferred political tactic of public pursuasion, they marched in the streets and lobbied in the halls of government. The Association's participation in the massive 1978 ERA march in Washington, D.C., marked not so much a rediscovery of feminism as a discovery of political action. If street demonstrations by civil rights workers or antiwar protesters had once appeared radical, by the 1970s public protests had become the tactic of choice for the entire political spectrum. Pro-ERA marchers, for example, regularly confronted those opposed to the amendment as both groups took their case to the streets. AAUW's presence in the pro-ERA demonstrations indicated not only the extent to which feminism had attracted a mainstream following but also the distance traveled by AAUW women in adopting the new political culture. According to one observer, some of the AAUW women who marched among fifteen hundred ERA supporters in Richmond, Virginia, "even wore pantsuits!"[66]

Members of AAUW and the women's movement worked tirelessly throughout the 1970s to secure passage of the ERA, but by 1974 only thirty-three states had ratified the amendment, and in 1977 five of those states voted to rescind their support.[67] Although feminist forces won a three-year extension of the ratification deadline in 1979, they were never able to win the support of enough states to secure the amendment's passage.[68] Nevertheless, AAUW, and the women's movement in general, emerged from the 1970s with a newfound legitimacy and an increasingly active constituency.

The 1970s marked many advances for women. Where, for example, in 1960 only 49 percent of women and 58 percent of men told a Gallop pollster they would vote for a woman for president, in 1984 a woman actually won the Democratic Party's nomination for vice president. According to one estimate, between 1970 and 1980 Congress "passed more bills that addressed women's issues than the sum total of all such bills passed in the previous history of the nation."[69] Legislative victories in employment rights, court rulings protecting reproductive rights, and affirmative action signaled a new legal status for American women. Equal opportunities finally appeared to be opening in education, in traditionally male professions, and in the political arena. Within AAUW, women felt a renewed sense of purpose. Contributions to the Educational Foundation were strong, support for AAUW programs remained enthusiastic, and the organization remained a respected component of the national women's rights community. By 1979 AAUW indeed defined the moderate mainstream of American feminism.

CONCLUSION

The women drawn to AAUW during the 1970s represented a new generation of feminists and an expanded constituency for women's organizations. If anything separated AAUW from its historical roots, it was this fact. More American women had college degrees, were employed, and pursued professions than at any time in the past. This change had profound implications for the culture of the women's movement, the strength of women's demands, and the issues on which feminist organizations focused. Even with this change in constituency, however, the fundamental nature of AAUW's feminism remained remarkably constant. Members continued to oppose hierarchies based on sex, to focus on education as a means of achieving equity, and to identify with a female-centered organization committed to advocating for women's rights.

Throughout the years, AAUW's unique contribution to the women's movement has been its focus on equity in education. When the organization expanded its membership criteria to encompass all women (and, ultimately, all people) with college degrees, it could legitimately claim to represent mainstream American women. Nothing could be more mainstream, after all, than the belief that education provides the key to equality in American life. For AAUW women, however, education has never simply represented a route to individual advancement or even to collective female achievement. Rather, it has signified a "badge of service," an obligation to use the privileges of higher education for broader social improvement.

At the root of AAUW's feminism is the belief that American institutions and American democracy have the capacity to provide equal opportunities for all citizens. Although it is true that AAUW members have opted to join a female-centered organization and have tended to believe that women have a special contribution to make to society, they also have believed that women deserve the same opportunities and respect as men. Their "family claim" has in no way implied that women possess lesser abilities than men or face diminished social responsibilities.

Modern feminism, however, does exist in tension with some of its older elements. Women were initially attracted to female-centered voluntary associations because they believed they could bring special talents and sensibilities to public service. They were also attracted to women's organizations because they were excluded from full participation in male-dominated institutions. Hence, women built a female culture that was characterized by self-motivated leadership and a self-confident spirit of achievement. By the end of the 1970s, however, individual women as well as women's organizations had increasing access to mainstream professional and political institutions. The sharp divide between women's culture and the dominant political culture was considerably narrowed. The problem facing women's organizations after 1980 was how to maintain an inner vitality and a volunteer spirit now that women had increasing opportunities to advance individually and contribute socially through mixed-sex groups. If it was a woman's culture that, at least in part, sustained women's organizations in the past, what would draw young women in the modern period into predominantly female associations now that they had achieved, or could hope to achieve, some level of equality? For AAUW, the answer lay, in part, in a reemphasis of its educational mission. The organization in the 1980s and early 1990s took the lead in identifying and suggesting measures for removing the stubborn barriers to educational equity that still existed for young girls in primary and secondary school, for women in college classes, and for minority women at all levels.

Changes in the strategic focus of AAUW's feminism also reflected a general transformation among American liberal social reform organizations. During the early part of the century, one of Progressive reform's central assumptions was that middle-class women would act for the general social good. Members of women's organizations such as AAUW also assumed that their demonstrated expertise would eventually convince lawmakers to remove the obstacles to women's equality. For years, AAUW and other organizations maintained their rosters of women qualified for public office in the belief that women's achievements would speak for themselves. The strategy followed by feminist organizations and women's groups alike was to convince policy makers, college administrators, and elected officials to find the right woman for the job. They were convinced that women's accomplishments— their competence as advisors, researchers, and mediators—would eventually convince lawmakers and the general public to end discrimination against women in public life. Unfortunately these tactics ultimately failed to bring large numbers of women into the mainstream of American political, educational, and economic institutions, and by the 1970s feminism's strategy for change had transformed dramatically.

With an expanded constituency of middle-class, college-educated women, organizations adopted grassroots strategies. They aggressively targeted issues and individuals and carried on public education campaigns, street demonstrations, and lobbying efforts. Feminists felt they were part of a mass movement in which the grass-roots pressure organizations could bring to bear on an elected official or a legislative vote would likely be more influential than the status or achievements of a single individual. As the activist climate of the 1960s waned, however, the center of political gravity shifted from local, volunteer-based organizations to national staff-centered operations. A new problem faced AAUW and reform movements generally: how to sustain the loyalty and commitment of their members in a political world increasingly populated by professionals working "inside the beltway." For AAUW, fellowship programs continued to provide a strong and unique source of allegiance, but enthusiasm for other programs was more difficult to sustain, particularly at the local level.

Ironically, adversity may well have provided fertile ground for AAUW and other organizations. Although the 1970s was an optimistic era of advancement for women, the 1980 presidential election and the inauguration of a new conservatism in the Reagan-Bush era signaled the fragility of many of women's public gains. A declining confidence in (and financial support for) public institutions, particularly schools, threatened to undermine many of the programs designed to ensure equal opportunity. In addition, legal and legislative rulings guarding civil rights and reproductive freedom were increasingly challenged. AAUW's voice in Washington and around the country became all the more important. Women whose college degrees promised equality still looked to AAUW to protect their gains and enable them to put their degrees to worthwhile use.

After a century of service, AAUW could proudly lay claim to a considerable influence upon the nation's history. Many doors previously closed to women were now open, thanks in large part to the unfailing efforts of this organized group of educated women. To be sure, new problems faced AAUW, and older obstacles remained. But if history is any judge, no group would be more likely to advance the standard of equity in education and the professional status of women than AAUW.

AFTERWORD

Alice Ann Leidel and Jackie DeFazio

The women who founded the American Association of University Women did so with a sense of urgency. They were deeply troubled by the social and economic barriers faced by women in gaining access to higher education and professional careers. They were also determined to make things better—to act and to have an impact. As college-educated activists and philanthropists they were dedicated to becoming catalysts for change, and they had faith in the concept that individuals working together could wield infinitely more influence than individuals working alone.

Through the years that philosophy has remained steadfast, and AAUW has worked to advance it on many fronts. We work to advance equity for women through the Association's political activism on local, state, and national levels. Through the Foundation's many fellowship and grant programs, largely funded by AAUW members, we help women develop knowledge and skills that, in turn, enable them to help other women and girls, while also bringing about positive changes in communities across the country. Through our Legal Advocacy Fund's awards and support for women in academia who have suffered sex discrimination, we further promote our historic mission. The critical factor behind our impact over our past century has been the strength of our grassroots efforts in AAUW branches in every state of the union.

Looking back, we realize that the longevity of our organization is remarkable in itself in a progressive society that accords considerably less reverence to tradition than it does to change. But our challenge has not been simply to endure, but to remain relevant by continuing to examine fundamental issues and taking appropriate, often innovative, action. If we are to achieve equity and education for all women and girls, we must constantly seek new ways to combat old problems.

Degrees of Equality traces the history of AAUW through 1980. In the years since, informed activism has continued to be our keynote. We gather information, study, and learn; then we act. By initiating sound research, we position ourselves to be heard and to be joined by others dedicated to strengthening our society by improving the opportunities for *all* women and girls regardless of race, creed, ethnicity, or economic standing. Individuals and organizations are joining with us to formulate policy and foster social change, and, increasingly in this multicultural society, we recognize that our impact comes from working in coalition with a diverse array of community groups and national organizations.

The late 1980s will, we believe, be viewed by future historians as a turning point for AAUW. Our focus sharpened in a way that reflected and expanded the vision of our founders. As other feminist organizations concentrated on a range of issues of interest to our organization and to all people concerned with women's rights, it became increasingly evident that our greatest successes could be achieved by concentrating on the subject we knew best: education and equity for women and girls—the women of tomorrow. In making this our focus we have not only promoted the groundbreaking work of researchers who are dedicated to gender equity in education, we have also provided the foundation for educators, political leaders, opinion makers, and members of the general public as they work to eliminate gender discrimination in our public schools.

In 1988, the AAUW Educational Foundation established the Eleanor Roosevelt Fund. Until that time, our funding was targeted almost exclusively to women in pursuit of post-baccalaureate degrees. As vital as this was—and continues to be—our focus is now on expanding opportunities more broadly by reaching girls in kindergarten through grade 12, girls just beginning their climb.

Today, the money raised for the fund by AAUW members are used for a 10-year research initiative and for the Eleanor Roosevelt Teacher Fellowship program, which trains experienced teachers in gender-fair teaching, techniques. The first piece of the research initiative was *Shortchanging Girls, Shortchanging America,* a 1991 nationwide poll conducted by Greenberg Lake: The Analysis Group, of girls and boys ages nine to 15. It assessed and related self-esteem, educational experiences, interest in math and science, and career aspirations and was the first study to link the sharp drop in self-esteem suffered by preadolescent girls to what they learned in the classroom.

The survey raised consciousness, and it also raised questions. How is it that most girls, who begin first grade with skills and ambitions comparable to those of boys, finish high school with a disproportionate loss of confidence in their academic abilities?

The Eleanor Roosevelt Fund followed up, commissioning the Wellesley College Center for Research on Women to compile and synthesize more than 1,300 documents about public school education for girls, from early childhood through college. *The AAUW Report: How Schools Shortchange Girls,* released in 1992, confirmed the prevalence and consequences of gender bias in school.

With *The AAUW Report* we learned, too, of the pervasiveness of sexual harassment in schools. This finding led to the commissioning of our 1993 Louis Harris poll. The resulting publication, *Hostile Hallways: The AAUW Survey on Sexual Harassment in America's Schools,* has, like *The AAUW Report,* served widely as a springboard to action.

Especially gratifying for AAUW members is the ripple effect of our work. Media attention about *Shortchanging Girls, Shortchanging America* inspired journalist Peggy Orenstein to spend a year with eighth-grade girls in two California schools. Her compelling book, *SchoolGirls: Young Women, Self-Esteem, and the Confidence Gap,* which puts human faces on AAUW statistics, was published in September 1994 by Doubleday.

Our research has sparked awareness about gender inequity in education, which in turn has lead to action—public forums and roundtables on the national, state, and local levels—and to teacher training and curriculum reform in schools across the nation.

Current and future AAUW Educational Foundation projects include a study of teaching techniques, methods, and programs that work for girls in school in grades K–12, and a national project called Girls Can!, a community/school partnership establishing gender-fair models in public schools across the country.

As the century draws to a close, AAUW continues to be an organization committed to making effective contributions toward ensuring an equitable place for all women and girls. Our history is a source of enormous pride, and we look forward to the future with great expectations. There is much to be done, and our commitment is long-term. In the words of Eleanor Roosevelt, *It is today that we must create the world of the future.*

NOTES

INTRODUCTION

1. Marion Talbot and Lois Kimball Mathews Rosenberry, *The History of the American Association of University Women: 1881–1931* (Boston: Houghton Mifflin, 1931), 421.

2. Nancy F. Cott, *The Grounding of Modern Feminism* (New Haven: Yale University Press, 1987), 4–5.

3. Attending the meeting were Anna E. F. Morgan, Ellen A. Hayes, and Margaret E. Stratton (who had graduated from Oberlin College); Ellen H. Richards, Florence M. Cushing, and Alice Hayes (Vassar); Lucy C. Andrews, Alice E. Freeman, and Mary O. Marston (University of Michigan); Mary H. Ladd (Cornell University); Maria M. Dean and Alma F. Frisby (University of Wisconsin); Sarah L. Miner and Marion Talbot (Boston University); S. Alice Brown (Smith College);and Harriet C. Blake and Edith E. Metcalf (Wellesley College). Talbot and Rosenberry, *History of the AAUW,* 9–10. For an account of the ACA and Marion Talbot, see Rosalind Rosenberg, *Beyond Separate Spheres: Intellectual Roots of Modern Feminism* (New Haven: Yale University Press, 1982), 18–27.

4. Although women accounted for about 20 percent of all college students in 1870, only 1 percent of American youth attended college. Rosalind Rosenberg, *Divided Lives: American Women in the Twentieth Century* (New York: Hill and Wang, 1992), 26.

5. M. Carey Thomas, "The Passionate Desire of Women . . . for Higher Education," in *Women's America: Refocusing the Past*, 3d ed., ed. Linda K. Kerber and Jane Sherron De Hart (New York: Oxford University Press, 1991), 296–297.

6. In Rosenberg, *Beyond Separate Spheres,* 5–12.

7. Rosenberg, Ibid., 19.

8. Ibid., 20.

9. Dorothy M. Brown, *Setting a Course, American Women in the 1920s* (Boston: Twayne, 1987), 35. On the details of Talbot's study, see Rosenberg, *Beyond Separate Spheres,* 20–24.

10. Rosenberg, *Beyond Separate Spheres,* 21–22.

11. Kate H. Claghorn, the first salaried secretary-treasurer, received one thousand dollars in 1898. Talbot and Rosenberry, *History of the AAUW,* 27.

12. Adelaide Stegman, "A History of the South Atlantic Region of the American Association of University Women," 1976 (manuscript). Courtesy, Adelaide Stegman.

13. Vera Hanawalt Frohlicher, *The Minnesota Division of the American Association of University Women: 1923–1953,* (AAUW, Minnesota State Division), 6. Courtesy, Ruth Hilland.

14. Barbara Miller Solomon, *In the Company of Educated Women: A History of Women and Higher Education in America* (New Haven: Yale University Press, 1985), 135.

15. Talbot and Rosenberry, *History of the AAUW,* 158–163.

16. Solomon, *In the Company of Educated Women,* 136.

17. Talbot and Rosenberry, *History of the AAUW,* 158–159. Rosenberg, *Beyond Separate Spheres,* 81.

18. "Evolution of the AAUW 'General Education' Requirement," AAUW Committee on Standards and Recognition Pamphlet, 1954, 2. AAUW original microfilm series, reel ED1, Associate Reports. (The AAUW archives contain microfilm reels that do not correspond to the circulating microfilm set.)

19. Stegman, "A History of the South Atlantic Region of the American Association of University Women."

20. Talbot and Rosenberry, *History of the AAUW,* 68.

21. "Evolution of the AAUW 'General Education' Requirement," 3–4.

22. Talbot and Rosenberry, *History of the AAUW,* 69.

23. Ibid., 71. (Emphasis in the original.)

24. Rosenberg, *Beyond Separate Spheres,* 44–45.

25. Solomon, *In the Company of Educated Women,* 79–85.

26. Talbot and Rosenberry, *History of the AAUW,* 72–73. The Association recognized the limited domestic opportunities for women in graduate education and in 1899 approved London University, Zurich Univer-

sity, the Sorbonne, "and all German universities which gave the Ph.D. degree to women."

27. Talbot and Rosenberry, *History of the* AAUW, 80.

28. See, for example, Ellen Fitzpatrick, *Endless Crusade: Women Social Scientists and Progressive Reform* (New York: Oxford University Press, 1990), and Lynn Gordon, *Gender and Higher Education in the Progressive Era* (New Haven: Yale University Press, 1990).

29. Talbot and Rosenberry, *History of the* AAUW, 207.

30. For a discussion of professional women, voluntarist politics, and feminism, see Cott, *Grounding of Modern Feminism*, chapter 7, passim.

31. Talbot and Rosenberry, *History of the* AAUW, 242.

32. Ibid., 242–257.

33. Southern Association of College Women, Durham Branch Minutes and Roll Book, 1913–1921, entry for October 1917, Durham Branch Records, Perkins Library Special Collections, Duke University.

34. On women's activities during World War I, see Brown, *Setting a Course*, 135, and Solomon, *In the Company of Educated Women*, 139. Although most ACA members favored, and even participated in, the suffrage movement, the Association did not take an official position on the question until 1919. Barbara A. Sokolosky, ed., AAUW *Archives, 1881–1975* (New York: Microfilming Corporation of America, 1980), 2.

35. Southern Association of College Women, Durham Branch Minutes and Roll Book, 1913–1921, entry for May 1921.

36. Talbot and Rosenberry, *History of the* AAUW, 37.

37. Ibid., 258–265.

38. AAUW *Journal*, January 1923, 1.

39. Ibid., June 1936, 236. The practice of bringing guests into the clubhouse became problematic after World War II when the Washington branch objected to black members using the headquarters' dining facilities. See Chapter 6.

40. AAUW *Journal*, June 1932, 228. AAUW branches, and other women's organizations, also opened clubhouses. The National Women's Party, for example, rented rooms in its national headquarters for overnight guests. See Susan D. Becker, *The Origins of the Equal Rights Amendment: American Feminism Between the Wars* (Westport, Conn.: Greenwood Press, 1981), 41.

41. Solomon, *In the Company of Educated Women*, 142. According to this source, women constituted 47.3 percent of total college enroll-

ments in 1920. The percentage declined after that, but the absolute numbers rose from about 283,000 in 1919–1920 to 480,000 in 1930.

42. Maude Wood Park, "Organized Women and Their Legislative Program," Women's Joint Congressional Committee Pamphlet, 1925, 3, Box 386, Folder entitled "Women's Joint Congressional Committee, Miscellaneous Papers." AAUW Archives, Washington, D.C. (Material from the AAUW Archives hereafter identified by box and folder numbers.)

43. Cott, *Grounding of Modern Feminism*, 44. On the early years of the NWP, see Becker, *Origins of the ERA*, chapters 2 and 3, passim.

44. *AAUW Journal*, October 1924, 19.

45. Ibid., January 1925, 18.

46. Ibid., 19.

47. Ibid., 18.

48. Becker, *Origins of the ERA*, 224. AAUW took no official position on the ERA until 1929, when the convention voted to oppose it.

49. Rosenberg, *Divided Lives*, 73–74; Cott, *Grounding of Modern Feminism*, 97–99.

50. See, for example, Louise M. Young, *In the Public Interest: The League of Women Voters, 1920–1970* (New York: Greenwood Press, 1989), 45.

51. *General Director's Letter*, December 15, 1934, 5–11 (hereafter cited as GDL). Also see Thomas Woody, *A History of Women's Education in the United States*, v. 2, (New York: Science Press, 1929), 464.

52. Harriet Hyman Alonso, *The Women's Peace Union and the Outlawing of War* (Knoxville: University of Tennessee Press, 1989), xiv. Also see Brown, *Setting a Course*, 65–66; Gertrude Bussey and Margaret Tims, *Pioneers for Peace: The Women's International League for Peace and Freedom, 1915–1965* (London: WILPF British Section, 1980); Catherine Foster, *Women for All Seasons: The Story of the Women's International League for Peace and Freedom* (Athens: University of Georgia Press, 1989).

53. Cott, *Grounding of Modern Feminism*, 244. Also see Memorandum on the Action and Attitude of the International Federation of University Women in Regard to the Nationality of Women, 1928–1933, AAUW microfilm reel 105. (Material in the AAUW circulating microfilm collection hereafter referred to by reel number.)

54. Cott, *Grounding of Modern Feminism*, 243.

55. Obituary in the *Washington Post*, July 9, 1965, Box 726, Folder 70.

56. Brown, *Setting a Course*, 56–57; Cott, *Grounding of Modern Feminism*, 98–99. Cott pointed out that the Cable Act also stipulated that if a

woman married a foreigner "ineligible by race for naturalization" (e.g., Chinese), she would still have to give up her own citizenship. Interestingly, some women, including Jane Addams, feared that the Act would be detrimental to the status of immigrant women. Young, *In the Public Interest,* 75. Also see Cott, *Grounding of Modern Feminism,* 98–99 and 265.

57. Memorandum on the Action and Attitude of the International Federation of University Women in Regard to the Nationality of Women, 1928–1933, Reel 105.

58. Talbot and Rosenberry, *History of the AAUW,* 417.

59. "American Association of University Women, 1929–1949," Reel 53.

60. Talbot and Rosenberry, *History of the AAUW,* 139.

61. Ibid., 137–142.

62. Ibid., 169–170.

63. *AAUW Journal,* May 1925, 12.

64. Dorothy Bridgman Atkinson, "Cornerstones of the Association," Box 727, Folder 136.

65. *AAUW Journal,* June 1931, 172. Also, Woolley told Elizabeth Fuller Jackson that the office of general director was "instituted to relieve the terrific pressure on the national president." Elizabeth Fuller Jackson to Lyda Bishop, October 13, 1939, Durham Branch Records, President's Files, 1939–1941.

66. Kathryn McHale, Report to the Board of Directors, 1935. Reel 1.

67. Mrs. A. W. Cooper to Kathryn McHale, April 24, 1931, Reel 49.

68. Ibid.

69. "Dr. Kathryn McHale," Memo to AAUW Board, National Officers, n.d. Reel 53.

PART I

1. "Dr. Susan M. Kingsbury," AAUW Archives, Washington, D.C., Box 726, Folder 128.

CHAPTER 1

1. Barbara Miller Solomon, *In the Company of Educated Women: A History of Women and Higher Education in America* (New Haven: Yale University Press, 1985), 172.

2. *AAUW Journal,* June 1939, 225.

3. Ware, *Holding Their Own,* 73.

4. *AAUW Journal,* June 1939, 225.

5. Cott, *Grounding of Modern Feminism,* 238.

6. McHale to Woolley, March 27, 1935, AAUW microfilm reel 48. (Material in the AAUW circulating microfilm collection hereafter referred to by reel number.) Until the late 1960s Association presidents all held Ph.D.'s.

7. Quoted in a letter from Elizabeth Fuller Jackson to Lyda Bishop, October 13, 1939, Durham Branch Records, President's Files, 1939–1941. Perkins Library Special Collections, Duke University. (Hereafter cited as Durham Branch Records.)

8. *AAUW Journal,* June 1932, 234.

9. Marion Talbot to Kathryn McHale, March 18, 1934, Reel 2.

10. In 1933 she reorganized the office "to develop the varied activities of the Association as a unified whole." "AAUW, 1929–1949," Reel 1.

11. Kathryn McHale to Mary Yost, December 12, 1934, Reel 49.

12. *AAUW Journal,* June, 1932, 234, and *General Director's Letter,* May 31, 1935, 1 (hereafter cited as *GDL*).

13. *GDL,* February 9, 1935, 5.

14. Kathryn McHale, "A Progress Report of AAUW Program Activities for 1933–1935," 4, Reel 1.

15. *AAUW Journal,* October, 1933, 1.

16. Clipping, n.d., n.p., and obituary in *Washington Post,* March 22, 1967, Box 726, Folder 76.

17. *AAUW Journal,* June 1937, 199.

18. Margaret Morriss to Kathryn McHale, February 5, 1937, and reply, February 16, 1937, Reel 48.

19. "Margaret Shove Morriss '48H," March 1975, Box 728, Folder 70.

20. Cott, *Grounding of Modern Feminism,* 234.

21. Marion Talbot and Lois Kimball Mathews Rosenberry, *The History of the American Association of University Women: 1881–1931* (Boston: Houghton Mifflin, 1931), 91.

22. Ibid., 76.

23. *AAUW Journal,* June 1936, 227.

24. Carrie B. Wilson, *History of the North Carolina State Division of AAUW* (Greensboro: Riser Printing Co., 1948), 12

25. Kathryn McHale to Mrs. Charles J. Oviatt, n.d., Reel 51.

26. Minutes, North Carolina Division, 1935–1937, 3 (n.d. for entry), Durham Branch Records.

27. Dorothy B. Atkinson Rood, "A Million Dollars for Fellowships—Yesterday, Today and Tomorrow," June 1953, Box 727, Folder 136.

28. Dorothy Bridgman Atkinson, "Cornerstones of the Association," Box 727, Folder 136. Also Ruth W. Tyron, *Investment in Creative Scholarship: A History of the Fellowship Program of the American Association of University Women, 1890–1956*, (Washington, D.C.: AAUW, 1957),188–191.

29. Quoted in Solomon, *In the Company of Educated Women*, 171. (Emphasis in the original.)

30. See Cott, *Grounding of Modern Feminism*, chapter 7.

31. *AAUW Journal*, October 1930, 23.

32. *GDL*, December 1934, 2.

33. Louise Franklin Bache to Kathryn McHale, April 6, 1939, SW AAUW Reels. Also see Susan D. Becker, *The Origins of the Equal Rights Amendment: American Feminism Between the Wars* (Westport, Conn.: Greenwood Press, 1981), 139.

34. Wilson, *History of the North Carolina State Division*, 13–14.

35. *GDL*, May 31, 1935, 1.

36. Becker, *Origins of the ERA*, 139.

37. See Susan Ware, *Beyond Suffrage: Women in the New Deal* (Cambridge, Mass.: Harvard University Press, 1981), 23–25.

38. *AAUW Journal*, June 1937, 202.

39. Kathryn McHale, "A Progress Report of AAUW Program Activities for 1933–1935," 30, Reel 1.

CHAPTER 2

1. Kathryn McHale, "A Progress Report of AAUW Program Activities for 1933–1935," 30, reel 1. (Material in the AAUW curculating microfilm collection hereafter referred to by reel number.)

2. Susan Ware, *Holding Their Own: American Women in the 1930s* (Boston: Twayne, 1982), 94.

3. Ibid., 101. Ware quoted Clark Chambers, "The lines of influence . . . worked both ways, from voluntary associations to public service and back."

4. McHale, "Progress Report of AAUW Program Activities," 4, Reel 1.

5. See, for example, *General Director's Letter*, December 15, 1934 (hereafter cited as *GDL)*.

6. Kathryn McHale to Georgette Waters, April 16, 1935, Reel 51. On opportunities for women opened up by the New Deal, see Ware, *Holding Their Own*, 89–97.

7. See, for example, "Report of the Program Committee for 1935–36," and "Report of the North Carolina Division, 1933–36." Also see "Branch President's Report, 1937–38," Durham Branch Records, President's Files, 1935–1937 Perkins Library Special Collections, Duke University. (Hereafter cited as Durham Branch Records.)

8. Kathryn McHale to Mrs. A. S. Heineman, Los Angeles, November 19, 1935, Reel 52; see also Susan D. Becker, *The Origins of the Equal Rights Amendment: American Feminism Between the Wars* (Westport, Conn.: Greenwood Press, 1981), 198–224.

9. GDL, April 10, 1934, 1.

10. McHale often published a column entitled "Some Feminist Notes" in the GDL. See, for example, November 1, 1933, 10. See also Becker, *Origins of the ERA*, 59.

11. Kathryn McHale to Mrs. A. S. Heineman, Los Angeles, November 19, 1935, Reel 52.

12. Minutes, Meeting of the Committee on the Economic and Legal Status of Women, April 13, 1934, 1. Also see Becker, *Origins of the ERA*, 224, and chapter 6, passim.

13. "Dr. Susan M. Kingsbury," AAUW Archives, Washington, D.C., Box 726, Folder 158. (Material from the AAUW Archives hereafter identified by box and folder numbers.)

14. Susan M. Kingsbury to Kathryn McHale, January 27, 1938, Reel 118; Memo to the Board of Directors Meeting, November 8–11, 1938, "Opposition to the Equal Rights Amendment," Reel 117.

15. Memo to the Board of Directors Meeting, November 8–11, 1938, "Opposition to the Equal Rights Amendment," Reel 117. Also see Frances Speek to Irene T. Heineman, May 4, 1939, Reel 118. Speek wrote of the need to prepare for a fight over the ERA at the convention. She expected the major pro-ERA forces to come from the National Women's Party.

16. See Ware, *Holding Their Own*, 107–111. For a discussion of women's political networks during the New Deal, see Susan Ware, *Beyond Suffrage: Women in the New Deal* (Cambridge, Mass.: Harvard University Press, 1981).

17. See Nancy F. Cott, *The Grounding of Modern Feminism* (New Haven: Yale University Press, 1987), chapter 7, passim. She argued that feminism and professionalism were essentially incompatible by the 1930s

and that most professional women eschewed feminism. AAUW women, on the contrary, strove to combine their professional ambitions with feminist commitment.

18. *AAUW Journal,* April 1937, 176.

19. Letter to members of the Committee on the Economic and Legal Status of Women from Susan M. Kingsbury, May 4, 1938, Reel 118.

20. Durham Branch Report of the Publicity Chairman, 1940–1941, Durham Branch Records, President's Files, 1939–1941.

21. Ware, *Holding Their Own,* 90.

22. Letter from Susan M. Kingsbury, Reel 118.

23. Ibid.

24. Kathryn McHale to members of the South Atlantic Sectional Conference, April 6, 1934, Reel 50.

25. "Status of Women Program" Historical Files (n.d.), AAUW original microfilm series. (The AAUW archives contain microfilm reels that do not correspond to the circulating microfilm set.) (Emphasis in the original.)

26. *GDL,* December 1934, 3.

27. "Annual Report of the North Carolina State Division, 1934–35," Durham Branch Records, President's Files, 1935–1937.

28. *GDL,* December, 1934, 3.

29. For an account of the Mount Holyoke controversy, also see Ware, *Holding Their Own,* 81.

30. Kathryn McHale to Mary Woolley, April 20, 1935, and Woolley to McHale, April 23, 1935, Reel 89. For an impressionistic account of the controversy, see Anna Mary Wells, *Miss Marks and Miss Woolley* (Boston: Houghton Mifflin, 1978), chapter 11.

31. Esther Brunauer to Edgar Furness, June 27, 1936, Reel 89.

32. Telegram to Ann Morgan from Kathryn McHale, n.d. (in reply to telegram from Morgan to McHale, April 26, 1935), Reel 89.

33. Woolley's relationship with Marks is discussed in Wells, *Miss Marks and Miss Woolley.* On the question of lesbianism among women during this period also see Ware, *Holding Their Own,* 64.

34. Kathryn McHale to Carolyn Smiley, February 10, 1937, Reel 89.

35. Esther Brunauer to Jeanette Marks, n.d., Reel 89.

36. Esther Caukin Brunauer to Dean Edgar Furness, June 27, 1936, Reel 89. McHale appears to have had a close personal involvement with Woolley and Marks. When Woolley died in 1947, Marks sent McHale Woolley's gold pin, which had deep significance for the three women. McHale was so distraught over Woolley's death that she was unable to offer much comfort to Marks. In a letter to Marks she lamented, "Many

people often say that time will heal these feelings, but I find that time exaggerates them." McHale to Marks, September 13, 1947, and October 16, 1947, Reel 89.

37. Kathryn McHale to Virginia Gildersleeve, December 16, 1936, Reel 89.

38. Meta Glass to Kathryn McHale, December 31, 1936, Reel 48. Also see Becker, *Origins of the* ERA, 224.

39. Carrie B. Wilson, *History of the North Carolina State Division of* AAUW (Greensboro: Riser Printing Co., 1948), 5. Vera Hanawalt Frohlicher, The Minnesota Division of the American Association of University Women: 1923–1953 (AAUW, Minnesota State Division), 25. Courtesy, Ruth Hilland.

40. Ware, *Holding Their Own*, 7. Also see Lynn Gordon, *Women's Bodies, Women's Rights* (New York: Penguin, 1976), chapters 10 and 11.

41. Ware, *Holding Their Own*, 103–105.

42. Because the Association was experiencing some economic difficulties that year, the convention proceedings were not transcribed.

43. Sister M. Madeleva to Kathryn McHale, September 15, 1935, Reel 109.

44. Mother M. Angelique to Kathryn McHale, August 28, 1935, Reel 109.

45. Kathryn McHale to Mrs. F. H. Waters, September 25, 1935, Reel 109.

46. Kathryn McHale to Sister Thomas Aquinas, August 28, 1935, Reel 109.

47. Sister M. Columkille to Kathryn McHale, November 5, 1935, Reel 109.

48. Meta Glass to Kathryn McHale, October 15, 1936, Reel 48.

49. Ruth Tyron to Kathryn McHale, August 15, 1935, Reel 109.

50. Apparently the southern California bishop also "advised his flock not to belong to such ungodly organizations." Mabel Merwin to Kathryn McHale, October 28, 1935, Reel 51.

51. Georgette Waters to Meta Glass, June 12, 1935, Reel 48.

52. Mrs. F. H. Waters to Kathryn McHale, October 11, 1935, Reel 51.

53. Clara Painter to Kathryn McHale, n.d., (November 1935), Reel 51.

54. "Iowa Division, AAUW, State Executive Board Meeting, November 2, 1935," Reel 109.

55. Mabel D. Merwin to Kathryn McHale, October 28, 1935, Reel 51.

56. Sally Spensley Michner to Kathryn McHale, August 15, 1935, Reel 109.

57. Bess Faxau to Kathryn McHale, November 25, 1935, Reel 109.

58. "Iowa Division, AAUW, State Executive Board Meeting, November 2, 1935," Reel 109.

59. The National Women's Party took no official stand on birth control, although some members opposed it. See Becker, *Origins of the ERA,* 256.

60. Minutes, AAUW Board of Directors, November 17, 1936, 4, Reel 109.

61. Esther Brunauer to Grace Hadow, October 9, 1936, Reel 48. Also Kathryn McHale to Carroll K. Michner, August 27, 1935, Reel 109.

62. Minutes, AAUW Board of Directors, November 17, 1936, "Report of the Special Committee on Legislation," Reel 109.

63. Meta Glass to Mrs. Edwin Every Park, December 21, 1936, Reel 48.

CHAPTER 3

1. See Nancy F. Cott, *The Grounding of Modern Feminism* (New Haven: Yale University Press, 1987), 243–267.

2. See Susan D. Becker, *The Origins of the Equal Rights Amendment: American Feminism Between the Wars* (Westport, Conn.: Greenwood Press, 1981), 129.

3. Anna Mary Wells, *Miss Marks and Miss Woolley* (Boston: Houghton Mifflin, 1978), 213.

4. Ibid., 220.

5. Minutes, AAUW International Relations Committee (hereafter IR), October 21, 1935, 1, AAUW microfilm reel 104. (Material in the AAUW circulating microfilm collection hereafter referred to by reel number.)

6. Wells, *Miss Marks and Miss Woolley,* 160.

7. *General Director's Letter,* December 1933, 13 (hereafter cited as GDL).

8. Ibid.

9. Esther Brunauer, "Thoughts on National Socialism and Popular Culture," n.d. (c. 1934), Reel 1.

10. GDL, December 1933, 19.

11. Ibid., 14.

12. Ibid., February 1934, 2.

13. Memo, Esther Caukin Brunauer, n.d., Reel 109.

14. Gladys Murphy Graham to Kathryn McHale, June 18, 1940, Reel 52.

15. "The Refugee Shop" of the Asheville, North Carolina Branch, February 11, 1941. Reel 109; Esther Brunauer to the Board of Directors, May 18, 1940, Reel 109; Carrie B. Wilson, *History of the North Carolina State Division of AAUW* (Greensboro: Riser Printing Co., 1948), 22.

16. Minutes, War Relief Committee, September 13, 1940, Reel 109. The War Relief Committee appears to have been made up principally of members of the Board of Directors. See *GDL*, April 17, 1942, 17.

17. "To the Presidents of State Divisions and Branches" from Margaret Morriss, June 21, 1940, Durham Branch Records, President's Files, 1939–1941 Perkins Library Special Collections, Duke University. (Hereafter cited as Durham Branch Records.)

18. Susan Lynn, *Progressive Women in Conservative Times: Racial Justice, Peace, and Feminism, 1945 to the 1960s* (New Brunswick, N.J.: Rutgers University Press, 1992), 22.

19. *AAUW Journal*, October 1938, 40.

20. Esther Brunauer to Mrs. Frederick Beggs, April 24, 1939, Reel 105. Also see Esther Brunauer, "Notes on My Experiences in Germany, 1933," Reel 1.

21. Minutes, IR, December 15, 1939, 3, and June 27, 1940, Reel 1.

22. Esther Brunauer to Mrs. Frederick Beggs, May 14, 1941, Reel 105. On women's organizations and the question of neutrality, see Lynn, *Progressive Women*, 22 and 97–103. Also see Susan M. Hartmann, "Women's Organizations During World War II: The Intersection of Class, Race, and Feminism," in *Women's Being, Women's Place: Feminism, Identity, and Vocation in American History*, ed. Mary Kelley (Boston: G. K. Hall, 1977), 313–328.

23. Kathryn McHale to Dera Parkinson, March 14, 1944, Reel 49.

24. Harriet Connor Brown to Esther Caukin Brunauer, March 14, 1940, Reel 105.

25. "Major Achievements of the AAUW, 1941–1943," 7, Reel 1; *GDL*, April 17, 1942, 1.

26. *GDL*, April 17, 1942, 2.

27. Ibid., 1.

28. Memo to Presidents of State Divisions and Branches from Margaret S. Morriss, June 20, 1940, Reel 148.

29. Wilson, *History of the North Carolina State Division*, 23–25.

30. *GDL*, April 17, 1942, 39. On military commissions for women, see *GDL*, January 1, 1942, 11.

31. E. T. James, J. W. James, and P. S. Boyer, *Notable American Women: A Biographical Dictionary*, s.v. "Virginia Gildersleeve" (Cambridge, Mass.: Belknap Press, 1971); Helen Dwight Reid to Agnes Ellen Harris, October 26, 1951, Reel 51. Also see Susan M. Hartmann, *The Home Front and Beyond: American Women in the 1940s* (Boston: Twayne, 1982), 35–36.

32. Hartmann, *Home Front,* 147.

33. Frances Valiant Speek to Helen C. White, January 19, 1944, Reel 48.

34. Ibid.

35. Ibid.

36. Ibid. Also see "Judge Lucy Somerville Howorth," AAUW Archives, Washington, D.C., Box 726, Folder 126. (Material from the AAUW Archives hereafter identified by box and folder numbers.)

37. See discussion of AAUW integration in Chapter 6.

38. Elizabeth Fuller Jackson to Lyda Bishop, April 4, 1941, Durham Branch Records, President's Files, 1939–1941.

39. Minutes, AAUW Committee on the Economic and Legal Status of Women (hereafter CELSW), January 24, 1941, and May 23, 1941, Status of Women. AAUW original microfilm series. (The AAUW archives contain microfilm reels that do not correspond to the circulating microfilm set.) Also Esther Brunauer to Mrs. Frederick Beggs, August 29, 1941, Reel 105.

40. Helen White to Kathryn McHale, April 29, 1943, Reel 48.

41. Open Letter from Frances Valiant Speek, Secretary to CELSW, July 27, 1942, Reel 118.

42. *GDL*, April 17, 1942, 38.

43. "Dr. H. C. White Explains Work for Housewives," *Washington, D.C., Sunday Star,* June 16, 1946. Also see other clippings in Box 728, Folder 109.

44. Hartmann, *Home Front,* 145.

45. Ibid., 149.

46. Ibid., 128.

47. Kathryn McHale to Sarah T. Hughes, November 6, 1942, Reel 118. (Emphasis in the original.)

48. Obituary, *New York Times,* April 25, 1985, Box 726, Folder 127.

49. "Judge Sarah T. Hughes," Box 726, Folder 127.

50. Helen C. White to Sarah T. Hughes, June 10, 1945, Reel 118.

51. Ibid.

52. Kathryn McHale to Sarah T. Hughes, April 28, 1947, Reel 118.

53. Minutes, CELSW, December 3, 1946, 5, Reel 117.
54. Minutes, CELSW, January 7, 1944, 1, SW AAUW Reels.
55. Leila J. Rupp and Verta Taylor, *Survival in the Doldrums: The American Women's Rights Movement, 1945 to the 1960s* (New York: Oxford University Press, 1987), 62. Also see Cynthia Harrison, *On Account of Sex: The Politics of Women's Issues, 1945–1968* (Berkeley: University of California Press, 1988), chapter 1, passim, and Hartmann, *Home Front,* 129–134.
56. Report of the Chairman, Committee on the Status of Women, December 3, 1946, 6. Reel 117.

PART II

1. See, for example, Leila J. Rupp and Verta Taylor, *Survival in the Doldrums: The American Women's Rights Movement, 1945 to the 1960s* (New York: Oxford University Press, 1987); Susan M. Hartmann, *From Margin to Mainstream: American Women and Politics Since 1960* (New York: Knopf, 1989); Rosalind Rosenberg, *Divided Lives: American Women in the Twentieth Century* (New York: Hill and Wang, 1992); Eugenia Kaledin, *Mothers and More: American Women in the 1950s* (Boston: Twayne, 1984); and Blanche Linden-Ward and Carol Hurd Green, *Changing the Future: American Women in the 1960s* (New York: Twayne, 1993).

CHAPTER 4

1. Nancy F. Cott, *The Grounding of Modern Feminism* (New Haven: Yale University Press, 1987), 248–251.
2. Minutes, AAUW Committee on the Economic and Legal Statues of Women (hereafter CELSW), February 3, 1939, 4, Status of Women. AAUW original microfilm series. (The AAUW archives contain microfilm reels that do not correspond to the circulating microfilm set. Hereafter cited as AAUW reels.) The Dies Committee also tried to impeach Labor Secretary Frances Perkins.
3. Ibid., 4–7. AAUW Reel 117. (Material in the AAUW circulating microfilm collection hereafter referred to by reel number.)
4. Margaret Morriss to Kathryn McHale, February 8, 1939, Status of Women, AAUW Reels.

5. *General Director's Letter,* December 16, 1940 (hereafter cited as GDL).

6. George Brown Tindall, *America: A Narrative History,* 2d ed. (New York: W. W. Norton, 1988), 1209.

7. Ibid., 1212.

8. Obituary, *New York Times,* October 10, 1956. AAUW Archives, Washington, D.C., Box 728, Folder 33. (Material from the AAUW Archives hereafter identified by box and folder numbers.)

9. Kathryn McHale to Mary B. Boyette, March 17, 1952, Reel 2.

10. Memorandum to the Board of Directors from the General Director (regarding "recent statements in the press referring to AAUW and Esther Caukin Brunauer"), November 28, 1952, 3, Reel 89.

11. Esther Brunauer, "Thoughts on National Socialism and Popular Culture," n.d. (c. 1934), Reel 1. Also see her papers, "National Socialist Youth in Germany," *English Journal* 24 (March 1935), and "Notes on My Experiences in Germany," mss. 1933, both in Reel 1.

12. Memorandum to the Board of Directors from the General Director, November 28, 1952, 2, Reel 89.

13. Esther Caukin Brunauer to Kathryn McHale, July 15, 1948, Reel 1.

14. Ibid., July 20, 1948, Reel 1.

15. Affidavit of Dr. Kathryn McHale, General Director, American Association of University Women, July 24, 1958, Reel 1.

16. Memorandum to the Board of Directors from the General Director, November 28, 1952, 2–3, Reel 89.

17. Susan M. Hartmann, *The Home Front and Beyond: American Women in the 1940s* (Boston: Twayne, 1982), 156, and Leila J. Rupp and Verta Taylor, *Survival in the Doldrums: The American Women's Rights Movement, 1945 to the 1960s* (New York: Oxford University Press, 1987), 138.

18. Hartmann, *Home Front,* 156. Also Rupp and Taylor, *Survival in the Doldrums,* 137–139.

19. GDL, April, 1950, 3.

20. Gretta A. Burchfield to Helen Bragdon, January 4, 1950, Reel 89.

21. "AAUW President Calls for Faith to Overcome Fears of Our Time," Press Release, n.d. (1951), Reel 2.

22. Statement by Dr. Ina Corinne Brown at a Meeting of the Board of Directors, November 30, 1950, Reel 89.

23. Ibid.

24. *Hollywood, Calif., Citizen News,* January 7, 1953, Box 728, Folder 16.

25. *AAUW Georgia Division Bulletin,* April 1952.

26. *Minneapolis Tribune,* June 18, 1953, Box 727, Folder 129.

27. *Washington Post,* June 23, 1953, Box 727, Folder 129.

28. Clipping, n.d., Box 728, Folder 129.

29. *Tennessean Magazine,* Nashville, May 13, 1951, Box 728, Folder 129.

30. Ibid.

31. Minutes, AAUW Board of Directors, November 15–16, 1952, 123, Board of Directors, AAUW Reels.

32. *AAUW Journal,* January 1953, 67. (Emphasis in the original.)

33. Ibid., 67–69.

34. "A Statement on the Record of the AAUW," November 1954, Reel 89.

35. Memorandum to the Board of Directors from Althea Hottel, December 15, 1950, Reel 89.

36. Minutes, AAUW Social Studies Committee, October 25–26, 1953, 3, Reel 113.

37. Report of National Officers and Committees to Biennial Convention, April 9, 1951, 34, Board of Directors, AAUW Reels.

38. *GDL,* January 1953, 29.

39. Minutes, AAUW Social Studies Committee, October 25–26, 1953, 3–4, Reel 113.

CHAPTER 5

1. Barbara Miller Solomon, *In the Company of Educated Women: A History of Women and Higher Education in America* (New Haven: Yale University Press, 1985), 63–64.

2. Ibid., 197.

3. Minutes, AAUW Social Studies Committee, November 4–5, 1961, 21, AAUW microfilm reel 113. (Material in the AAUW circulating microfilm collection hereafter referred to by reel number.)

4. "Youth and Cupid Provide Surprises," *Los Angeles Times,* April 4, 1957, and Clipping (no source or date), "College and Cooking Can Mix," AAUW Archives, Washington, D.C., Box 726, Folder 39. (Material from the AAUW Archives hereafter identified by box and folder numbers.)

5. Leila J. Rupp and Verta Taylor, *Survival in the Doldrums: The*

American Women's Rights Movement, 1945 to the 1960s (New York: Oxford University Press, 1987), 50–52.

6. "Answers to Questionnaire for AAUW Members," 1956, Reel 122.

7. Ibid.

8. Report of the Chairman, Committee on the Status of Women, December 3, 1949, Reel 117.

9. Verbatim Transcript, AAUW Board of Directors, October 25, 1947, 16–17, Box 744, Folder 65. (This discussion hereafter referred to as Board Discussion, October 1947.)

10. Ibid., 18–19.

11. Susan Riley to Melanie R. Rosborough, February 11, 1954, Reel 50.

12. Mrs. S. C. McKee to the Board of Directors, November 9, 1951, Reel 51.

13. *Mitchell, S.D., Daily Republic,* April 18, 1958, Box 726, Folder 100.

14. "New Women's Bureau Assistant," n.d. (1954), Box 726, Folder 107.

15. Eugenia Kaledin, *Mothers and More: American Women in the 1950s* (Boston: Twayne, 1984), 44.

16. Report of the Chairman, Committee on the Status of Women, January 24, 1948, Reel 117.

17. Board Discussion, October 1947, 51–53.

18. Ibid., 49–50.

19. Ibid., 57.

20. Report of the Associate in Higher Education to the National Education Committee, November 9, 1944, 2, Higher Education, AAUW original microfilm series. (The AAUW archives contain microfilm reels that do not correspond to the circulating microfilm set.)

21. Susan M. Hartmann, *The Home Front and Beyond: American Women in the 1940s* (Boston: Twayne, 1982), 106.

22. Ibid., 107.

23. Solomon, *In the Company of Educated Women,* 198. Also see Hartmann, *Home Front,* 106–107.

24. Solomon, *In the Company of Educated Women,* 191.

25. Hartmann, *Home Front,* 107.

26. Solomon, *In the Company of Educated Women,* 189.

27. Ibid., 188–189. Also see Eugenia Kaledin, *Mothers and More,* 53.

28. Solomon, *In the Company of Educated Women,* 193.

29. Board Discussion, October 1947, 40.

30. *Wyoming Morning Star,* May 5, 1953, Box 727, Folder 7.

31. *Mitchell, S.D., Daily Republic,* April 18, 1958, Box 726, Folder 100.

32. Report of the Chairman, Committee on the Status of Women, January 24, 1947, 1, Reel 117. Also see Kaledin, *Mothers and More,* 49.

33. *Mitchell, S.D., Daily Republic.*

34. Clipping from Omaha, Nebr., newspaper, no title, April 15, 1958, Box 726, Folder 100.

35. AAUW News Release, "Dr. Anna L. Rose Hawkes Dies," October 10, 1978, Box 726, Folder 100.

36. Board Discussion, October 1947, 43.

37. AAUW, *Idealism at Work: Eighty Years of AAUW Fellowships* (Washington, D.C.: AAUW, 1967) 294.

38. Ibid., 297.

39. Frances Concordia, interview with author, Portland, Oreg., June 1991. Also see "Frances Butler (Mrs. Charles) Concordia," Box 725, Folder 94.

40. Concordia interview.

41. Concordia interview. Also see "AAUW Milestones," 1981, Box 519, Folder entitled "AAUW History," and Minutes, AAUW Board of Directors, February 18–19, 1961, 8, Box 744, Folder 74.

42. Concordia interview.

43. AAUW, *Idealism at Work,* 297.

44. Ibid., 305.

45. Ibid., 312.

46. See annual reports from the chairman of the Committee on the Status of Women, Reel 117.

47. See Cynthia Harrison, *On Account of Sex: The Politics of Women's Issues, 1945–1968* (Berkeley: University of California Press, 1988), chapter 4, passim.

48. See Rupp and Taylor, *Survival in the Doldrums,* 66.

49. Memo to Helen D. Bragdon and Gertrude H. Harris from Elizabeth G. Holt on Notes of Status of Women Office, June 1955, 6, Reel 117.

50. Althea Kratz Hottel to President Truman, September 15, 1950, Reel 117.

51. Verbatim Transcript, AAUW Board of Directors, November 1–3, 1945, 101, Box 744, Folder 62.

52. Minutes, AAUW Committee on the Status of Women, February 28–March 1, 1942, 2, Reel 117.

53. Hartmann, *Home Front,* 149. She also pointed out that the "overall percentage of women in elective office remained small."

54. Harrison, *On Account of Sex,* 64.

55. Verbatim Transcript, AAUW Board of Directors, November 1–3, 1945, 89–92, Box 744, Folder 62.

56. Minutes, AAUW Committee on the Status of Women, October 30, 1951, 2, Reel 117.

57. See, for example, Rosamonde Ramsay Boyd to Governor Adlai Stevenson and Boyd to General Dwight D. Eisenhower, August 18, 1952.

58. Minutes, International Relations Committee, May 23–24, 1953, 6, Reel 104.

59. Hartmann, *Home Front,* 130.

60. Rosamonde R. Boyd to Winifred G. Helmes, February 13, 1952, Reel 118.

61. Ibid., August 29, 1952, Reel 118.

62. Ibid., September 10, 1952, Reel 118. (Emphasis in the original.)

63. Ibid., February 13, 1952, August 25, 1952, and September 10, 1952, Reel 118.

64. See *General Director's Letter,* January, 1953, 23–25.

65. Clipping from the *St. Paul Pioneer Press,* June 25, 1953, Box 407, Folder entitled "ERA–AAUW."

66. Kaledin, *Mothers and More,* 99.

67. Gertrude Fariss to Elizabeth Holt, June 2, 1955, Reel 118.

68. "Gertrude Houk Fariss (Mrs. Crecene A.)," AAUW Press and Radio Information, Box 726, Folder 37.

69. Gertrude Fariss to Frances T. Freeman Jalet, n.d., Reel 119.

70. "AAUW Hears Warning on Women's Status," unidentified clipping from Washington State, 1958, in Farris biographical file, Box 726, Folder 37.

71. Gertrude Fariss to Nancy Jewel Cross, January 8, 1955, Reel 118.

72. Minutes, AAUW Committee on the Status of Women, November 23–25, 1956, 7–8, Reel 117.

73. Gertrude Fariss to Dorothy McCullough Lee, April 27, 1957, Reel 117.

74. Gertrude Fariss to Mrs. Frances Tucherman Freeman, May 20, 1957, Reel 119.

75. Frances Jalet to Gertrude Fariss, August 2, 1957, Reel 119.

76. Gertrude Fariss to Frances Jalet, August 9, 1957, Reel 119.

77. Ysabel Forker to Mrs. Earl A. Frederickson (Carmen), January 16, 1959, Reel 119.

78. Ellen Winston to Ysabel Forker, January 20, 1959, Reel 119.

79. "AAUW Proposed Dues Increase," June 10, 1966, 3, Reel 49.

80. Nancy Douglas Joyner, "AAUW's Structural Evolution in Perspective," October 21, 1978. Courtesy, Dorothy Sponder.

CHAPTER 6

1. See Leila J. Rupp and Verta Taylor, *Survival in the Doldrums: The American Women's Rights Movement, 1945 to the 1960s* (New York: Oxford University Press, 1987), 156.

2. Susan Lynn, *Progressive Women in Conservative Times: Racial Justice, Peace and Feminism, 1945 to the 1960s* (New Brunswick, N.J.: Rutgers University Press, 1992), 46–49.

3. Susan M. Hartmann, *The Home Front and Beyond: American Women in the 1940s* (Boston: Twayne, 1982), 148. Also Lynn, *Progressive Women,* 46, and Louise M. Young, *In the Public Interest: The League of Women Voters, 1920–1970* (New York: Greenwood Press, 1989), 172.

4. Kathryn McHale to Mary Louise Barnes, September 23, 1941, AAUW microfilm reel 86. (Material in the AAUW circulating microfilm collection hereafter referred to by reel number.)

5. Ibid., Reel 51.

6. Kathryn McHale to Mrs. H. K. Painter, March 16, 1943, and McHale to Arthur A. Guild, September 26, 1945, Reel 51. Also see "Memorandum for the Board of Directors," December 4, 1946, Reel 86. This memo lists black membership by state.

7. Kathryn McHale to Mary Louise Barnes, September 23, 1941, Reel 86.

8. Kathryn McHale to Leonore W. Thomas, April 5, 1939, Reel 86.

9. Kathryn McHale to Mrs. Charles D. Crawford, November 10, 1941. Also see Kathryn McHale to Leonore W. Thomas, April 5, 1939, Reel 86.

10. Kathryn McHale to Mrs. Charles D. Crawford, November 10, 1941, Reel 86.

11. Kathryn McHale to Mary Louise Barnes, September 23, 1941, Reel 86.

12. Kathryn McHale to Leonore W. Thomas, April 5, 1939, Reel 86.

13. Ibid.

14. Kathryn McHale to Mary Louise Barnes, September 23, 1941, Reel 86.

15. Memo, Ruth Wilson Tyron to Kathryn McHale, December 5, 1941, Reel 86.

16. Mary Smith to Kathryn McHale, December 5, 1941, Reel 86.

17. Mrs. Charles D. Crawford, to the AAUW, November 1, 1941, Reel 86.

18. Letter addressed to Martha Sawyer enclosed in note to her from Mrs. Replinger, February 24, 1942, Reel 86.

19. Alice L. Meadows to Kathryn McHale, December 2, 1941, Reel 86.

20. Marion R. Draper to Marion B. Werner, April 8, 1943, Reel 86.

21. Marion B. Werner, California State Division, to Esther Cole Franklin, April 21, 1943, Reel 86.

22. Minutes, AAUW International Relations Committee, September 30, 1938, 1, Reel 104.

23. Kathryn McHale to Victoria Schuck, November 12, 1946, Reel 86.

24. *General Director's Letter,* January 1, 1942, 4 (hereafter cited as GDL).

25. GDL, December 1942, 20–21.

26. Mrs. H. K. Painter to Kathryn McHale, March 11, 1943, Reel 51.

27. D. D. P. to Kathryn McHale, July 20, 1943, Reel 86.

28. Elise W. Graupner (Mrs. A. E.), San Francisco, to Kathryn McHale, April 16, 1946, and her statement to the branch board of directors, February 13, 1945, Reel 86.

29. Mrs. Eugene M. Rial to Kathryn McHale, June 9, 1945, Reel 86.

30. Verbatim Transcript, AAUW Board of Directors, November 1–3, 1945, 155, AAUW Archives, Washington, D.C., Box 744, Folder 71. (Material from the AAUW Archives hereafter identified by box and folder numbers; the meeting referred to here is hereafter referred to as Board of Directors, November 1945.)

31. Elise W. Graupner (Mrs. A. E.), San Francisco, to Kathryn McHale, April 16, 1946, Reel 86.

32. Board of Directors, 1945, 163–164.

33. Ibid., 126 and 170.

34. Ibid., 153.

35. Ibid., 160.

36. Ibid., 155.

37. Ibid., 160.

38. Helen White to Gillie Larew, April 9, 1947, Box 845, Folder entitled "Correspondence, 1946–49-W."

39. Kathryn McHale to Victoria Schuck, Mount Holyoke, November 12, 1946, Reel 86.

40. Helen C. White to Gillie Larew, April 9, 1947, Box 845, Folder entitled "Correspondence, 1946–49-W." Also see Gillie Larew to Miss Clyde G. Carter, January 21, 1948, Reel 50.

41. Board of Directors, 1945, 158.

42. Susan Riley to Mrs. John H. Sweitzer, Nashville, Tenn., February 5, 1947, Reel 86.

43. "Facts About Mrs. Mary Church Terrell's Application for Membership in the Washington Branch, AAUW," October 24, 1946, Reel 86.

44. AAUW Convention Proceedings, Seattle, June 20, 1949, 88.

45. "To the Board of Directors of the American Association of University Women," April 8, 1947, Reel 86.

46. Minutes, AAUW Board of Directors, December 6–8, 1946, 13, Board of Directors, AAUW Reels.

47. "Dr. Althea Kratz Hottel." Courtesy, Dorothy Sponder.

48. Marion Talbot to Kathryn McHale, February 13, 1948, Reel 2.

49. "Dr. Althea Kratz Hottel." Courtesy, Dorothy Sponder.

50. GDL, February 1949, 1.

51. AAUW Convention Proceedings, Seattle, June 20, 1949, 4–6.

52. Elizabeth Conrad to the Washington Branch Members, in Minutes, AAUW Executive Committee, July 30, 1948, Box 139, Folder 2.

53. "An Informal Report on the Membership Problem in the San Diego Branch," by Virginia H. Lanphier, June 15, 1948, in Minutes, Executive Committee (n.p., n.d.), Board of Directors, AAUW original microfilm series. (The AAUW archives contain microfilm reels that do not correspond to the circulating microfilm set. Hereafter cited as AAUW reels.) Also see AAUW Convention Proceedings, Seattle, June 20, 1949, 195.

54. Owen J. Roberts to Althea Hottel, July 26, 1948, in Minutes, AAUW Executive Committee, July 30, 1948, Box 139, Folder 2.

55. *AAUW Journal*, Spring 1949, 131.

56. Susan Riley to Mrs. John H. Sweitzer, February 5, 1947, Reel 86.

57. *AAUW Journal*, Spring 1949, 133.

58. Minutes, AAUW Board of Directors, December 4–5, 1948, "Exhibit A-1," 14a, Board of Directors, AAUW Reels.

59. Ibid., April 9–10, 1948, 14-d, 14-e, Board of Directors, AAUW Reels.

60. Board of Directors, 1945, 166–167.

61. "An Informal Report on the Membership Problem in the San Diego Branch," by Virginia H. Lanphier, June 15, 1948, in Minutes, Executive Committee (n.p., n.d.), Board of Directors, AAUW Reels.

62. Mrs. Earl C. Rice, to Althea Hottel, April 30, 1948, Reel 86.

63. "An Informal Report on the Membership Problem in the San Diego Branch," by Virginia H. Lanphier, June 15, 1948, in Minutes, Executive Committee (n.p., n.d.), Board of Directors, AAUW Reels.

64. Virginia Lanphier to Helen S. Graves (Mrs. George S.), April 25, 1948, Reel 52.

65. Mary Smith to Virginia Lanphier, April 30, 1948, Reel 52.

66. Ina C. Brown, to Althea Hottel, July 10, 1950, Reel 48.

67. Ibid.

68. *AAUW Journal*, Winter 1947, 225.

69. Althea Hottel to Kathryn McHale, November 11, 1947, Reel 51.

70. *AAUW Journal*, Fall 1949, 23.

71. Rupp and Taylor, *Survival in the Doldrums*, 58. Also see *AAUW Journal*, Fall 1949, 32–33.

72. Susan Riley to the National Board of Directors, April 5, 1948, Reel 51.

73. Minutes, AAUW Board of Directors, November 30–December 1, 1950, 108, Board of Directors, AAUW Reels. For a brief discussion of the AAUW integration crisis, see Rupp and Taylor, *Survival in the Doldrums*, 156–158.

74. Minutes, AAUW Social Studies Committee, October 26–28, 1957, 4, Reel 113.

75. Minutes, Board of Directors Meeting, June 17–18, 1949, 95, Board of Directors, AAUW Reels.

76. Memo from Helen D. Bragdon to Mrs. Sherrard, March 25, 1954, Reel 116, and Memo from Lucy Howorth to Susan Riley and Helen Bragdon, September 19, 1954, Reel 116.

77. The discussion of integration in the Nashville branch is based on

"Integration Procedures in the Nashville Branch, AAUW," 1955 (marked "*Not* for general circulation or publication), Durham Branch Records, Unarranged files (Perkins Library Special Collections, Duke University. (Hereafter cited as Durham Branch Records.)

78. Ibid.

79. William H. Chafe, *Civilities and Civil Liberties: Greensboro, North Carolina, and the Black Struggle for Freedom* (Oxford: Oxford University Press, 1980), 31.

80. Minutes, Durham Branch Executive Board, November 21, 1955, Box M, Minutes of Executive Board 1954–1957, Durham Branch Records.

81. "Summary of Returns on Places of Meetings," November 21, 1955, Durham Branch Records, unarranged files.

82. Ibid.

83. Mrs. Carl A. Plonk to Miss Mamie Mansfield, October 20, 1955, and Helen D. Bragdon to Miss Mamie Mansfield, October 14, 1955, Durham Branch Records, unarranged files.

84. Helen D. Bragdon to Miss Mamie Mansfield, October 14, 1955, Durham Branch Records, unarranged files.

85. Florence Brinkley to Mrs. Derric A. Sherman, April 25, 1961, Durham Branch Records, President's Files, 1960–1961.

86. See Minutes, Durham Branch, October 4, 1955, through March 6, 1956, Durham Branch Records, Box M, Folder entitled "Branch Minutes."

87. Ibid.

88. George Brown Tindall, *America: A Narrative History,* 2d ed. (New York: W. W. Norton, 1988), 1331.

89. Minutes, AAUW Social Studies Committee, October 23–24, 1954, 5, Reel 113.

90. Memo from Lucy Howorth to Susan Riley and Helen Bragdon, September 19, 1954, Reel 116.

91. Minutes, AAUW Social Studies Committee, October 23–24, 1954, 21, Reel 113.

92. Memo from Lucy Howorth to Susan Riley and Helen Bragdon, September 19, 1954, Reel 116.

93. Minutes, AAUW Social Studies Committee, October 23–24, 1954, 21, Reel 113.

94. Susan Riley to Janet MacDonald, November 29, 1954, Reel 116.

95. Janet MacDonald to Nancy D. Lewis, chair of editorial committee, October 25, 1954, Reel 116.

96. Susan Riley to Edith Sherrard, October 15, 1956, Reel 116 (HST = Harry S. Truman).

97. Minutes, AAUW Social Studies Committee, October 23–24, 1954, 10, Reel 113.

98. Memo to State Division Presidents, South Atlantic Region, from Rosamonde Ramsay Boyd, March 23, 1955, Reel 116.

99. Ibid.

100. See Minutes, Durham Branch Board, September 6, 1956, Durham Branch Records, Box M, Folder entitled "Minutes of Executive Board, 1954–57." I thank Christina Greene for sharing this material with me. On the Pearsall Plan, see Chafe, *Civilities and Civil Liberties,* 53–60.

PART III

CHAPTER 7

1. Barbara Miller Solomon, *In the Company of Educated Women: A History of Women and Higher Education in America* (New Haven: Yale University Press, 1985), 63–64.

2. Ibid., and Blanche Linden-Ward and Carol Hurd Green, *Changing the Future: American Women in the 1960s* (New York: Twayne, 1993), 68.

3. Linden-Ward and Green, *Changing the Future,* 91.

4. Stephanie Coontz, *The Way We Never Were: American Families and the Nostalgia Trap* (New York: Basic Books, 1992), 163.

5. Ibid., and Linden-Ward and Green, *Changing the Future,* 93 (emphasis mine).

6. Linden-Ward and Green, *Changing the Future,* 340 and 396; Coontz, *The Way We Never Were,* 185–186.

7. Membership chart dated 1976 in Memo from Helen Wolfe to Harriet Maurer, June 3, 1976, AAUW Archives, Washington, D.C., Box 468, Folder 18. (Material from the AAUW Archives hereafter identified by box and folder numbers.)

8. Stenotypist's Report, AAUW Executive Committee, October 30, 1971, Box 139, Folder 15.

9. Data based on AAUW Member Assessment Study, December–January 1980–1981. Courtesy, Dorothy Sponder.

10. AAUW Member Assessment Study, December–January 1980–1981, Table 84. Courtesy, Dorothy Sponder.

11. Sarah Harder to "Morning Edition" Editor, National Public Radio, September 4, 1987, Box 516, Folder entitled "Byrant, CHRON—September."

12. Alice Beeman to Mrs. M. Margoshes, March 5, 1971, Box 502, Folder 7.

13. Ibid.

14. Verbatim Transcript, AAUW Board of Directors, October 22, 1977, 131–139, Box 27, Folder 43.

15. Linden-Ward and Green, *Changing the Future,* 83.

16. Anne Firor Scott, *Natural Allies: Women's Associations in American History* (Urbana: University of Illinois Press, 1993), 3.

17. *General Director's Letter,* April 1967, 2. Hereafter cited as GDL.

18. Josephina Cintron Tiryakian to Mrs. Gloria Blanton, April 25, 1975, Durham Branch Records, Box labeled "AAUW Received 3/1987," Folder entitled "AAUW Next Meeting." Perkins Library Special Collections, Duke University. (Hereafter cited as Durham Branch Records.)

19. "Structure Discussion," Stenotypist's Report, AAUW Board of Directors, June 24, 1961, Box 744, Folder 84.

20. "Blanche Hinman Dow," Box 726, Folder 15.

21. "Mrs. Hyatt Boyette, Staff Associate, Public Information, to Mrs. R. D. Peironnett, Kansas City, Mo., November 25, 1969, Box 726, Folder 15.

22. Virginia Watson, to Mary Boyette, May 15, 1973, Box 726, Folder 15.

23. GDL, April 1963, 1.

24. Mary Grefe, interview with author, Portland, Oreg., June 1991.

25. Linden-Ward and Green, *Changing the Future,* 67, 75–76, 81–82, and 121.

26. AAUW, *Idealism at Work: Eighty Years of AAUW Fellowships* (Washington, D.C.: AAUW, 1967), 3.

27. Ibid., 296–297.

28. Doris C. Davis, *Idealism at Work: AAUW Educational Foundation Programs, 1967–1981* (Billings, Mont.: AAUW, 1981), viii.
29. Stenotypist's Report, AAUW Educational Foundation, April 11, 1963, 12, Box 744, Folder 2.
30. Davis, *Idealism at Work*, ix.
31. Davis, *Idealism at Work*, ix.
32. Minutes, AAUW Educational Foundation Programs Committee, October 23, 1975, 6, Box 847, Folder 23.
33. Minutes, AAUW Fellowships Program Committee, November 21, 1970, 3, Box 847, Folder 33.
34. Stenotypist's Report, AAUW Educational Foundation, February 11, 1963, 17, Box 744, Folder 2.
35. Notes on Research and Projects Endowments, Box 469, Folder 50.
36. Davis, *Idealism at Work*, 383–384.

CHAPTER 8

1. See, for example, Blanche Linden-Ward and Carol Hurd Green, *Changing the Future: American Women in the 1960s* (New York: Twayne, 1993), 2–10; Susan M. Hartmann, *From Margin to Mainstream: American Women and Politics Since 1960* (New York: Knopf, 1989), 50–53; Flora Davis, *Moving the Mountain: The Women's Movement in America Since 1960* (New York: Simon and Schuster, 1991), 34–38. Also see Jane Sherron DeHart, "The New Feminism and the Dynamics of Social Change," in *Women's America: Refocusing the Past*, 3d ed., ed. Linda Kerber and Jane Sherron DeHart (New York: Oxford University Press, 1991), 495–521; and Rosalind Rosenberg, *Divided Lives: American Women in the Twentieth Century* (New York: Hill and Wang, 1992), 82–86.
2. Linden-Ward and Green, *Changing the Future*, 4–7.
3. Quoted in Davis, *Margin*, 36–37.
4. AAUW Resolutions, 1959–1961. Courtesy, Dorothy Sponder.
5. Durham Branch Report, 1961, Durham Branch Records, President's Files, 1960–1961. Also see "Durham Branch of AAUW, 1957–1967," 6, Durham Branch Records, History of Durham Branch. (Perkins Library Special Collections, Duke University. (Hereafter cited as Durham Branch Records.) Branch membership was back up to 76 in 1957 and ranged between 68 and 83 during the next decade.

6. "Minutes of the Convention of the North Carolina State Division," October 9–10, 1964, Durham Branch Records, President's Files, 1963–1965.

7. Hartmann, *From Margin to Mainstream,* 52. Also see Rosenberg, *Divided Lives,* 181–186.

8. Davis, *Moving the Mountain,* 37.

9. See Rosenberg, *Divided Lives,* 185–186.

10. Meta M. Haupt to Dorothy D. Button, September 25, 1972. Courtesy, Judy Knudsen.

11. "Activist Details Changes Facing American Women," *Buffalo Courier-Express,* October 9, 1980, AAUW Archives, Washington, D.C., Box 725, Folder 57. (Material from the AAUW Archives hereafter identified by box and folder numbers.)

12. Debra W. Stewart, *The Women's Movement in Community Politics in the U.S.: The Role of Local Commissions on the Status of Women* (New York: Pergamon, 1980), 13.

13. Elizabeth B. Stanton to Anne Pannell, May 21, 1968; Minutes, AAUW Executive Committee, Box 139, Folder 8.

14. Alice S. Rossi to Leslie W. Syron, August 26, 1969, Reel 119.

15. Ione Paradise to Alice Beeman, August 25, 1969, Reel 119.

16. "A Guide for A.A.U.W. Speakers," Status of Women Committee, San Fernando Valley Branch, 1961, Reel 2.

17. Adelaide Stegman to Elizabeth Hull, October 13, 1971, and reply, October 20, 1971, Reel 50. Also see Linden-Ward and Green, *Changing the Future,* chapter 11, passim. They argued "Rapidly changing dress styles through the sixties provide a measure of the transformation of attitudes of and about women; but changes often were more 'cosmetic' than real indices of social and economic status" (p. 319).

18. Linden-Ward and Green, *Changing the Future,* 410.

19. Ibid., 411. Also see Hartmann, *From Margin to Mainstream,* 56–66.

20. Dorothy R. Cutter to Sarah Harder, August 11, 1987, Box 519, Folder entitled "Washington, DC/EC." (Emphasis in the original.)

21. Mrs. Robert (Ione) Paradise to Alice Beeman, August 15, 1969, Reel 119.

22. Cynthia Harrison, *On Account of Sex: The Politics of Women's Issues, 1945–1968* (Berkeley: University of California Press, 1988), 94. For an example of AAUW's earlier lobbying for Congressional action on equal pay, see, Marjorie L. Temple to Winifred Helmes, September 10, 1951,

Reel 118, outlining the AAUW's continuing support for congressional legislation ensuring women equal pay for equal work.

23. Hartmann, *From Margin to Mainstream*, 59–61.

24. Leila J. Rupp and Verta Taylor, *Survival in the Doldrums: The American Women's Rights Movement, 1945 to the 1960s* (New York: Oxford University Press, 1987), 180–181.

25. Francena Miller to Eleanor B. Walters, April 15, 1968, Reel 51.

26. Stenotypist's Report, AAUW Executive Committee, June 13, 1969, 7, Box 139, Folder 9. Also see "Board-Staff Planning Session," n.d. (April 29, 1968), Reel 49.

27. "Dr. Anne Gary Pannell," December 1950, Box 728, Folder 98.

28. "In and Out of Washington," *McCalls,* May 1968, Clipping in Box 728, Folder 98.

29. *General Director's Letter,* April, 1969, 23.

30. The following is based on author's interview with Elise Smith, Portland, Oreg., June 1991.

31. "Elise Smith, Foundation Programs Committee," 1987. Courtesy, Dorothy Sponder.

32. Alice Beeman to Bea Dolan, May 11, 1970, Reel 119.

33. "Survey of Branch Educational Foundation Programs Chairmen," 1977–1978, Box 469, Folder 48.

34. Wanda Breese to Elaine Teletzke, May 1, 1975, Reel 50.

35. Alice Beeman to Josephine Morrison, March 12, 1970, Reel 50.

36. *Graduate Woman,* February/March 1986, 6.

37. Memo to the AAUW staff from Alison Bell, no date. Box 497, Folder 16. The results of the poll were: favoring the ERA, 53.8 percent yes, 44.5 percent no, 1.9 percent equivocal; on withdrawal from Vietnam, 66.07 percent yes, 30.6 percent no, 4.03 percent equivocal.

38. The LWV did not endorse the ERA until 1972. Louise M. Young, *In the Public Interest: The League of Women Voters, 1920–1970* (New York: Greenwood Press, 1989), 180ff.

39. Rosenberg, *Divided Lives,* 212; Hartmann, *From Margin to Mainstream,* 68.

40. Mrs. Ione Paradise to Alice Beeman, April 12, 1970, Reel 119.

41. "AAUW Legislative History and Policy Notes," 3d ed., 1981–1983, AAUW Public Policy Department Pamphlet, 1981, 28.

42. *Graduate Woman,* February/March 1986, 6.

43. *AAUW Journal,* March 1971, 6.

44. The following is based on author's interview with Anne Campbell, Portland, Oreg., June 1991.

45. *AAUW Journal,* March 1971, 6.

46. Campbell interview.

47. In 1956 there were nine regional vice presidents on the board. *Graduate Woman,* May/June 1979, 43.

48. Mrs. R. E. Niffenegger to Mrs. Jim Cherry, January 3, 1975, Box 407, Folder entitled "ERA-AAUW."

49. Eleanor Sanger Keys, "Fair Play," *Outlook,* Summer 1992, 19.

50. Kappy Eaton, interview with author, Portland, Oreg., June 1991.

51. Helen B. Wolfe, "American Association of University Women: A Second Adolescence," speech delivered at AAUW convention, June 27, 1977, Box 728, Folder 126.

52. Joyce Gelb and Marian Lief Palley, *Women and Public Policies* (Princeton: Princeton University Press, 1982), 20.

53. "ERA Committee," Handwritten notes, December 7, 1975, Box 469, Folder 64.

54. Memo to Board of Directors from ERA Ad Hoc Committee, February 17, 1976, Box 469, Folder 64.

55. See Donald G. Mathews and Jane Sherron DeHart, *Sex, Gender, and the Politics of ERA: A State and the Nation* (New York: Oxford University Press, 1990), 74–76. Also see Jane L. Mansbridge, *Why We Lost the ERA* (Chicago: University of Chicago Press, 1986).

56. Memo to Board of Directors from ERA Ad Hoc Committee, February 17, 1976, Box 469, Folder 64.

57. "AAUW Legislative History and Policy Notes," 3d ed., 1981–1983, AAUW Public Policy Department Pamphlet, 1981, 27.

58. "Equal Rights Amendment: Questions and Answers," Equal Rights Amendment Project, n.d. (1976), Box 469, Folder 64.

59. Ibid.

60. Judith Paterson, *Be Somebody: A Biography of Marguerite Rawalt* (Austin, Tex.: Eakin Press, 1986), 183.

61. Marjorie Bell Chambers, "From Puritan to Person," Speech delivered to the North Atlantic Regional Conference, September, 1975, Reel 1.

62. The following is based on author's interview with Marjorie Bell Chambers, Portland, Oreg., June 1991.

63. Chambers interview.

64. Helen B. Wolfe, "American Association of University Women: A

Second Adolescence," Speech delivered at AAUW convention, June 27, 1977, Box 728, Folder 126.

65. Ibid.

66. Memo to ERA Ad Hoc Committee from Anita Miller, January 16, 1976, Box 469, Folder 64.

67. Hartmann, *From Margin to Mainstream*, 137.

68. Rosenberg, *Divided Lives*, 227.

69. Davis, *Moving the Mountain*, 417.

Appendix A

AAUW Presidents

Ada L. Comstock, 1921–1923

Aurelia Henry Reinhardt, 1923–1927

Mary E. Woolley, 1927–1933

Meta Glass, 1933–1937

Margaret S. Morriss, 1937–1941

Helen C. White, 1941–1947

Althea K. Hottel, 1947–1951

Susan B. Riley, 1951–1955

Anna L. Rose Hawkes, 1955–1963

Blanche H. Dow, 1963–1967

Anne Gary Pannell, 1967–1971

Anne Campbell, 1971–1975

Marjorie Bell Chambers, 1975–1979

Mary A. Grefe, 1979–1980, President, Educational
   Foundation, 1985–1989

Mary H. Purcell, 1981–1985

Sarah Harder, 1985–1989

Sharon Schuster, 1989–1993

Alice McKee, President, Educational Foundation, 1989–
   1993

APPENDIX B

Table 1   College Women as a Percentage of All Young
Women in the United States

Year	Percentage
1880	1.9
1900	2.8
1920	7.6
1940	12.2
1960	15.4
1980	37.9

Source: Barbara Miller Solomon, *In the Company of Educated Women:
A History of Women and Higher Education in America* (New Haven: Yale
University Press, 1985), 64. *Note:* The age range was 18 to 21 until 1950
and 18 to 24 thereafter.

Table 2   Women as a Percentage of All College Students

Year	Percentage
1880	33.4
1900	36.8
1920	47.3
1940	40.2
1960	37.9
1980	51.8

Source: Barbara Miller Solomon, *In the Company of Educated Women:
A History of Women and Higher Education in America* (New Haven: Yale
University Press, 1985), 63.

Table 3   AAUW Membership (Total Dues-Paying Members)

Year	Membership Total
1922–1923	16,433
1929–1930	35,579
1939–1940	68,003
1949–1950	112,746
1959–1960	143,601
1969–1970	165,586
1975–1976	190,327

Source: Compiled from AAUW membership files, AAUW archives, Washington, D.C.

INDEX